The Internet in Brazil

in Brazil

Origins, Strategy, Development, and Governance

PETER T. KNIGHT

authorHOUSE®

AuthorHouse™ LLC
1663 Liberty Drive
Bloomington, IN 47403
www.authorhouse.com
Phone: 1-800-839-8640

Published by AuthorHouse 05/01/2014

ISBN: 978-1-4918-7248-2 (sc)
ISBN: 978-1-4918-7247-5 (hc)
ISBN: 978-1-4918-7246-8 (e)

Library of Congress Control Number: 2014904794

Contents

List of Figures and Tables

Figures

Tables

Glossary of Acronyms

ADSL	Asymetric Digital Subscriber Line
Anatel	National Telecommunications Agency
Aneel	National Electric Energy Agency
ANSP	Academic Network at São Paulo
APC	Association for Progressive Computing
ARPA	Advanced Research Projects Agency (US)
BBS	Bulletin Board System
BITNET	Because It's Time Network
BRICS	Brazil, Russia, India, China and South Africa
CETIC.br	Center of Studies on Information and Communication Technologies
CGI.br	Brazilian Internet Steering Committee
CIA	Central Intelligence Agency (US)
CNPq	National Council for Scientific and Technological Development
DARPA	Defense Advanced Research Projects Agency (US)
DEPIN	Department of Informatics and Automation Policy, MCT
DNS	Domain Name System
FAPESP	São Paulo Research Foundation
FAPERJ	Rio de Janeiro Research Foundation
FINEP	Financing Agency for Studies and Projects
Fistel	Telecommunications Supervision Fund
FTTx	Fiber to the Home, Curb, Premises, etc.
Funttel	Fund for Development of Telecommunications Technologies

Fust	Fund for Universalization of Telecommunications Services
Gbps	Gigabits per second
Gesac	Electronic Government - Citizens' Support Service
Ghz	Gigahertz
GVT	Global Village Telecom
IANA	Internet Assigned Numbers Authority
IBASE	Brazilian Institute for Social and Economic Analyses
IBGE	Brazilian Institute of Geography and Statistics
ICANN	Internet Corporation for Assigned Names and Numbers
ICMS	Tax on Circulation of Goods and Delivery of Services
ICT	Information and Communications Technologies
IDI	ICT Development Index
IETF	Internet Engineering Task Force
IGC	Institute for Global Communication
IGF	Internet Governance Forum
IMF	International Monetary Fund
ISOC	Internet Society
ISP	Internet Service Provider
ITU	International Telecommunications Union
LARC	National Computer Network Laboratory
LGT	General Telecommunications Law
LNCC	National Laboratory for Scientific Computing
LTE	Long Term Evolution
Mbps	Megabits per second
MC	Ministry of Communications
MCT	Ministry of Science and Technology
MCTI	Ministry of Science, Technology, and Innovation

MIT	Massachusetts Institute of Technology
Mhz	Megahertz
NIC.br	Brazilian Network Information Center
NRI	Network Readiness Index
NSA	National Security Agency (US)
NTIA	National Telecommunications and Information Administration (US)
NSF	National Science Foundation (US)
OPGW	Optical Ground Wire
OSI	Open Systems Interconnection
PGMC	General Plan for Competition Goals
PNAD	National Household Sample Survey
PNBL	National Broadband Plan
PoP	Point of Presence
PPB	Basic Production Process
PUC-Rio	Catholic University of Rio de Janeiro
REDLAC	Latin American Computer Network
RNP	National Research and Education Network, originally National Research Network
RST	Southern Teleprocessing Network
SCM	Multimedia Communication Service
SEI	Special Secretariat for Informatics
SPB	Brazilian Payments System
TCP/IP	Transmission Control Protocol/Internet Protocol
UFRGS	Federal University of Rio Grande do Sul
UFRJ	Federal University of Rio de Janeiro
UNCED	United Nations Conference for Environment and Development
UNESP	São Paulo State University
Unicamp	State University of Campinas
USP	University of São Paulo

UNESCO	United Nations Education, Science and Cultural Organization
WCIT	World Conference on International Communications
WEF	World Economic Forum
WSIS	World Summit on the Information Society
3G	Third Generation wireless technology
4G	Fourth Generation wireless technology

Preface

By Vint Cerf[*]

The book you are reading is an important contribution to the history of the Internet, in particular, in Brazil. There are several reasons why this is such a valuable contribution. First, Brazil has grown to become among the most prosperous and influential countries, not only in Latin America, but on the world stage. The way in which Brazil has managed the introduction of the Internet contains useful lessons for the rest of the Internet Community.

The Brazilian Internet Steering Committee (CGI.br) is responsible for overseeing and aiding Internet development in the country. In order to perform its activities, the CGI.br created a non-profit civil organization, the Brazilian Network Information Center (NIC.br) that provides a range of services to the Brazilian Internet community as is illustrated in its web site, http://www. cgi.br/english/activities/index.htm, and discussed in Chapter 7 of this book.

But what is most important about CGI.br is the multistakeholder model that it has successfully implemented for the formulation, adoption and execution of policy regarding the Internet in Brazil.

---

[*] **Vint Cerf** is widely known as a "Father of the Internet". He was co-designer of the TCP/IP protocols that govern packet information flows and of the basic architecture of the Internet. He was a founder of the Internet Society and its first president as well as chairman of ICANN from 2000-2007. He is currently Vice President and Chief Internet Evangelist of Google.

The CGI.br includes the federal government, the private sector, civil society, and the technical and academic communities. At a time when there is much tension between governments and others in the Internet community over policy, this example serves as a reminder of what is possible.

The history of the Internet in Brazil begins in the academic community, as has been common for many countries, including the United States, where the Internet was first implemented. It has expanded in scale and in access over a period of decades, heavily assisted by the development of mobile smartphones and by optical fiber networks that bring high speed and critical connectivity to the country. To this we can add the existence of Internet eXchange Points (IXPs) and multiple Internet Service Providers. All of these technologies and the businesses that make them available contribute to the vitality of the Internet in Brazil.

The high tech protectionism of the 1980s has given way to a much more vibrant and international economy and this has created an atmosphere in which entrepreneurs have thrived. The universities are turning out well-educated graduates in technical and business disciplines and these feed a growing number of new companies whose business needs create new jobs that contribute to the economy.

Over the past four years, beginning with a statement ten basic principles elaborated by CGI.br, a highly participatory debate involving all sectors of the Brazilian Internet community has taken place to develop legislation called the Civil Rights Framework for the Internet. Extensive crowdsourcing over the Internet, public hearings and seminars, and debate in Congress contributed to the drafting process. Both its content and the process by which it was elaborated are worthy of study by other countries and the international Internet community.

I hope that other chroniclers, like Peter Knight, will take the time and effort to help us understand the way in which Internet is received and nurtured in the many other countries of the world. In the meantime, I hope you will find this book as interesting as I have.

Foreword

This book expands on a more journalistic article entitled "The Internet in Brazil: Poor strategy weakens progress" in B*raudel Papers* No. 48, a publication of the Fernand Braudel Institute of World Economics in São Paulo.[1] I had to keep that article to about 8,000 words to meet space limitations. But I wanted to write a longer, more academic piece with complete documentation and references for readers interested in a deeper exploration of the subject matter.

My passion for the Internet and its enormous potential for accelerating economic, social and political development dates back to 1992 when I was leading an external training unit of the World Bank dealing with national economic management. One day John Gage, then of Sun Microsystems, walked into my office and showed me the Mosaic web browser and the World Wide Web. Later he introduced me to one of Russia's ICT pioneers, Sasha Galitsky. I never looked back and two years later founded the Bank's Electronic Media Center. In 1994, with Galitsky, who had led a team controlling Soviet Union spy satellites, and three of his colleagues, I presented a paper at the Second International Conference on Distance Education in Russia.[2]Galitsky is now an international venture capitalist

After that first meeting with John, I had opportunities to interact with him at various conferences. I have also been influenced by many other Internet pioneers over the last 20 years. I am especially indebted to one of them, Vint Cerf – a true father of the Internet and long-time source of encouragement – for writing the preface to this book. John Gage, George Sadowsky, Larry Landweber, Steve Goldstein, Spartak Belyaev, Sasha Galitsky, Yuri Hohlov, Tatiana Ershova, Nancy Hafkin, Hisham el Sherif, Mike Jenson, Venancio Massingue, Demi Getschko, Michael Stanton, Tadao Takahashi, Ivan Moura Campos, and many other Internet pioneers from many countries also inspired my work.

On one occasion, a conference in the World Bank, I recall John Gage getting up and telling the then President of that institution, James Wolfensohn: "Mr. President, I have only one recommendation to make. In any World Bank financed project that involves digging (sewers, pipelines, railways), put in optical fiber. Fiber is cheap, and digging is expensive. This is a low-cost investment with very high returns." That spurred my interest in "future-proof" fiber optic networks that should be evident in this book.

I have worked many years on Brazil in various organizations since doing research for my Ph.D. dissertation here in 1967-68 and meeting my Carioca wife, Zaida. In 2000 the Second Global Forum on eGovernment was held in Brasília, and I decided to participate. President Fernando Henrique Cardoso (FHC) and an old friend, Pedro Parente, head of FHC's civilian staff (*Ministro da Casa Civil*), spoke. I made a number of contacts there, and two years later, together with three other eGovernment enthusiasts, assembled a team of some 40 specialists to write a book on eGovernment in Brazil and the world that was published in 2004.[3]

Under the new administration of President Luiz Inácio da Silva (Lula) the priority given to eGovernment fell, but there was a new emphasis on digital inclusion of the population, albeit with few resources being allocated to achieve this objective and weakly coordinated programs in various ministries. Seeking to build national support for an overarching multi-sector national eDevelopment strategy to take advantage of the ICT revolution, two Brazilian colleagues (one from the government, Ciro Fernandes, one from academia, Alexandra Cunha) and I launched the *e-Brasil* project. We mobilized a team of 70 specialists, including some from abroad who wrote chapters on relevant experience in other countries.

This team included professionals holding posts in the Lula government and others from FHC's second administration, state governments, academia, the private sector, and civil society organizations. The team spanned a wide range of political and ideological perspectives. We held an international conference in 2005 and produced two books, covering both eDevelopment strategy and applications in a wide range of government and private sector activities. One was launched before the 2006 elections.[4] The second, a larger and more complete version with 40 chapters, was published with the support of the Brazilian Chamber of e-Commerce in 2007.[5] Both were widely distributed. The second was launched in the Congress in 2007 and won a coveted Jabutí prize from the Brazilian Chamber of Books in 2008.

The impact of the *e-Brasil* project on government policies is hard to assess. Nevertheless, one member of the team was a member of President Lula's staff, and another was the Secretary of Logistics and Information Technology in the Ministry of Planning. The latter, Rogério Santanna, was a major author of the National Broadband Program initiated at the end of President Lula's second administration discussed in some detail in Chapter 5 of the present book. He later became the first President of Telebras, the principal instrument for implementing the National Broadband Program in the administration of President Dilma Rousseff. Perhaps their participation in the e-Brasil project and the distribution of the book within government circles had some influence. It's hard to say. The *e-Brasil* project was an initiative of our diverse team, not of the government.

But the primary objective of the *e-Brasil* project, the development of a holistic eDevelopment strategy for Brazil, that we now call an eTransformation strategy, has yet to be achieved. Disappointed with this result, I became more involved in comparing Brazil's experience with that of other countries and drawing some general conclusions to guide future efforts. I and my former World Bank colleague and eTransformation guru, Nagy Hanna, were editors and participating authors of two books covering a total of eight countries, published in 2011 and 2012.[6]

In Brazil I became an active participant in the development of fiber optic networks, working on projects in the states of Acre, Ceará and Rio de Janeiro in close contact with the National Education and Research Network (*Rede Nacional de Ensino e Pesquisa* – RNP). I saw RNP as a valuable partner for states seeking to build or expand their own networks. I believe that the rapid expansion of fiber optic networks will provide the indispensable infrastructure needed to support the transformative advanced applications the e-Brasil team advocated to accelerate the country's economic, social, and political development as well as to improve its competitiveness in international markets.

When Norman Gall, Executive Director of the Braudel Institute, asked me to write a long article on the Internet in Brazil for *Braudel Papers*, I accepted, again with a view to promoting development of an eTransformation strategy and the ICT infrastructure to support it. The present book is an extension of that effort that seeks to document what has been achieved to date and to suggest what remains to be done.

The support of the Braudel Institute leadership and staff was instrumental in motivating and supporting my work. I would like to thank innumerable Brazilian and international colleagues for their contributions to my own knowledge and development. For this book I owe a special gratitude to Vint Cerf for writing the preface and to Carlos Afonso, Guilherme Almeida, Marcelo Bechara, Norman Gall,Nagy Hanna, Fred Morris, João Moura, and Michael Stanton, who read and commented on drafts.

Alexandre Barbosa facilitated access to CETIC.br survey data. Artur Coimbra, Ludmila Ribeiro and Pedro Araújo helped me obtain copies of important studies conducted for the Ministry of Communications. Basílio Perez and Breno Vale at the Brazilian Association of Internet and Telecommunications Providers (Abrint) introduced me to small and medium providers whom I call Internet Pioneers (Bandeirantes da Banda Larga). Michael Stanton, Theo Pires, Leila Daher, and Fernando Carvalho contributed network maps. And Vint Cerf secured permission to use Figure 11 on the Internet Governance Ecosystem. Tyler Elliott and Robert DeGroff of AuthorHouse guided me through an accelerated editorial process. Of course the responsibility for any errors of fact or interpretation are mine alone. Thanks also to my wife, Zaida, for her support in proof reading, and for putting up with my intense effort over the past months as I researched and wrote the article and now the book. Of course the responsibility for any errors of fact or interpretation is mine alone.

Peter T. Knight

Founding member, researcher, and
member of the Board of Directors

Fernand Braudel Institute of World Economics

Rio de Janeiro, April 2014

Foreword

1   Knight (2013).
2   Galitsky et al. (1994).
3   Chahin, Cunha, Knight & Pinto (2004)
4   Knight & Fernandes (2006)
5   Knight, Fernandes & Cunha (2007).
6   Hanna & Knight (2011 and 2012).

Chapter 1

The Strategic Importance of the Internet for Brazil's Development

Both Brazilians and international observers are prone to contradictory views of Brazil's future. An Austrian immigrant, Stefan Zweig, coined the expression "Brazil, a Country of the Future" the title of an insightful book published in 1941.[1] On a more pessimistic note, Brazilians often say that Brazil is the country of the future, and always will be. During the military dictatorship (1964-1985), propaganda boasted that "Brazil was the country of the future, but now the future has arrived", an optimistic expression repeated by United States President Barak Obama during a visit to Rio de Janeiro in 2011.

At the beginning of 2014 the mood is more somber. Economic growth has been anemic over the past three years, inflation is on the rise, and the Brazilians' evaluation of their own politicians had reached a new low.[2] In June 2013, millions of demonstrators, largely mobilized over the Internet, took to the streets in cities around the country to protest corruption, impunity, and poor public services. Many expect that mass protests of this kind will be repeated during the World Cup soccer matches to take place in June and July 2014.

In April, before the World Cup, another, less publicized international event was hosted in Brazil, the Global Multistakeholder Meeting on the Future of Internet Governance, also dubbed NETmundial. Brazil has been a leader in developing and implementing

1

multistakeholder governance of the Internet, where government, private sector, academia, civil society organizations and Internet professionals perform this function. Brazil's model of Internet governance, embodied in the Brazilian Internet Steering Committee (*Comitê Gestor da Internet no Brasil* – CGI.br), was held up as a possible model for other countries and for international Internet governance during NETmundial.

In 2009, Brazilians began preparing legislation, called the Civil Rights Framework for the Internet (*Marco Civil da Internet*) that establishes principles, guarantees, rights and obligations for the use of the Internet in Brazil. This legislation was closely studied by participants in NETmundial. But the process by which this legislation has been developed may also be seen as a model for other countries and indeed for the international institutions involved in Internet governance. This process has been thorough, highly participatory, democratic, and has made ample use of the Internet (websites, wikis, blogs, social networks, etc.). It may herald a new, more modern mode of policy making – something of which Brazilians can be proud.

This book examines how the Internet came to Brazil, how it has developed, how it is governed, and why its future development is strategic for achieving national goals. This chapter deals with the last of these issues, presenting arguments for putting the Internet at the center of Brazil's strategy for achieving better future.

Background: Brazil in a nutshell

Brazil is the largest and arguably the most important country in Latin America. With an estimated population of 202 million in February 2014, it is also the most populous. In 2012 Brazil's economy was the seventh largest in the world according to four separate estimates by the United Nations, the IMF, the World Bank, and the CIA, ranging from US$ 2.3 to 2.4 trillion.[3] Per capita income was US$11,354 in 2012, or 60th highest in the world according to the IMF, well above China's US$6071, but half of South Korea's.

Brazil also has well-known weaknesses. Though income inequality as measured by the Gini coefficient (running from zero for perfect equality to 1 for absolute inequality) has fallen from .57 in 1997 to .50 in 2012 according to the official Brazilian statistical agency, it is still a serious problem.[4] Of the BRICS countries, only South Africa has a higher degree of income concentration, according to both the United Nations and CIA estimates for the latest years available.[5] Other broad indicators put Brazil way down in the rankings. For example, the World Economic Forum's (WEF) competitiveness ranking for Brazil in its 2013-2014 report was 56 out of 148 countries, though it was the best of the BRICS countries except for China, ranked 29th. South Korea ranked 25th.[6] The WEF competitiveness index includes a very wide range of sub-indicators covering national policies, institutions, and factors affecting productivity (e.g. education, health, innovation, and infrastructure).

The Internet and the information and communications revolution

The Internet is a great invention of the 20th Century that is changing the civilization of the 21st Century. Its power grows with the fiber optic cables that are now the nerves of the world economy. No other technology permits greater speed of transmission nor generates greater economies of scale at such a low cost as fiber optic cables. Thanks to this worldwide system of storing, organizing and sharing information, 90% of the data that exists in the world today was created over the past two years. In 2012, every day 2.5 quintillion bytes (exabytes – that is 1 followed by 18 zeros) of data were created.[7] Meanwhile, in June 2013, the number of Internet users reached 2.4 billion, 34% of the world's population, an increase of 566% since the year 2000.[8]

This enormous flood of data is expected to double every two years through 2020, propelled by the increase in Internet users and their increasing consumption and production of video, among other factors.

Figure 1: The Digital Universe

50-fold Growth from the Beginning of 2010 to the End of 2020

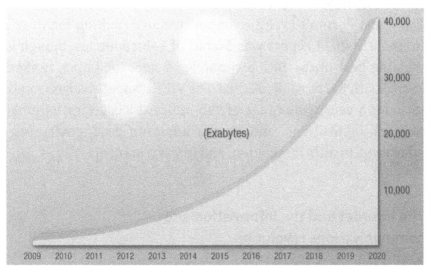

Source: Ganz & Reinsel (2013)

The Internet has become the world's most important means of processing information, comparable to the invention of the printing press with moveable type by Johannes Gutenberg, that has expanded access to the printed word and the horizons of human knowledge since the 15th century. In that time paper and ink were fundamental. Today the physical means of communication are fiber optic cables, supplemented by satellites and terrestrial wireless technologies. Extending over land, under oceans or in space, together they are creating the essential infrastructure of the 21st century.

Fiber optic cables and the rapidly expanding processing power of computers are reshaping economies worldwide. Packets of information, data, text, voice and image are sent over these cables, reduced to zeros and ones transmitted over the Internet using TCP/IP (Transport Control Protocol/Internet Protocol). Combined with other information and communication technologies (ICT),[9] the Internet is a tool with multiple uses that strengthens economic and social development as well as political participation. More and more, all forms of electronic communication – including telephony, Internet, radio and television – are being transmitted over the Internet on fiber optic cables.

Brazil has to move fast to accompany these developments. The Internet's growth in Brazil is being encouraged by federal, state and municipal governments, incumbent and insurgent telecommunications companies in large and medium-sized cities, and small Internet service providers (ISPs) that I call broadband pioneers. These small ISPs have played an important role in digital inclusion of the population, including in remote areas of the country that face many challenges.

The huge increase in the processing power of chips, and the devices that contain them (computers, tablets, smartphones, etc.), has drastically reduced the cost of transmitting, processing, and storing data, making knowledge cheaper and more accessible throughout the world. Communication based on the Internet

5

protocols is rapidly substituting the older technologies and the business models based upon them.

While the cost of processing, transmitting, and storing data has fallen at an exponential rate, the amount of data created has exploded, facilitated by this fall in costs. Change is so rapid that institutions have been unable to keep up. Advanced systems, such as biotechnology and nanotechnology, depend on ICT. Strategies based on this wave of technological change have become critical in shaping the competitiveness and even survival of individuals, businesses, cities, and nations.

This wave of change empowers people and organizations to leap ahead of competitors that fail to adopt these strategies. The advent of ICT is an example of the "waves of creative destruction" that the great economist Joseph Schumpeter (1883-1950) analyzed in his book *Capitalism, Socialism and Democracy.* [10] Because of this creative destruction, growth of traditional telephony has slowed throughout the world, with use declining in some countries. Much voice traffic already flows over the Internet. A large part of this traffic comes from traditional telephone companies, but an increasing portion is generated by computer-based software such as Skype, Viber and WhatsApp.

Meanwhile, mobile devices have proliferated. Globally the number of mobile phones already exceeded the number of fixed line phones in 2002. By the end of 2012 they reached 6.8 billion for a penetration rate of 96.2% of global population,[11] compared with 1.2 billion fixed line phones, and the number of fixed line phones is declining as many people "cut the wire" and rely on mobile phones.[12] Mobile phone penetration globally is expected to pass 100% of population in 2013.

But estimates of the number of unique mobile subscribers vary from 4.5 to 5.9 billion, since many subscribers have more than one mobile phone or a phone with more than one number (separate SIM card) to take advantage of special offers or coverage of different operators. Also, mobile operators are often slow to remove inactive lines.[13] According to ICT consultancy Gartner, global smartphone sales to end users reached 968 million in 2013, a 42% increase over 2012, and for the first time accounting for over half of all mobile phones sold.[14] That makes 2013 smartphone sales almost double the 494 million shipped in 2011. This rapid growth is now driven largely by the sales of cheaper models, priced as low as US$50 in China.[15]

Mobile devices, led by smartphones, are producing an explosive increase in wireless data traffic — set to rise by some 300% by 2017 to a peak of 21 Exabytes, from just 5 Exabytes in 2012. Driving that rise are services like streaming video.[16]

Video is very data-intensive compared with text, graphic, and even audio traffic. Globally, Internet video traffic is projected to be 69 percent of all consumer Internet traffic in 2017, up from 57 percent in 2012. This percentage does not include video exchanged through peer-to-peer (P2P) file sharing. The sum of all forms of video (TV, video on demand, Internet, and P2P) is projected to be in the range of 80 to 90 percent of global consumer traffic by 2017.[17]

Benefits of an eTransformation strategy

Intensive use of ICT should be a central strategy to accelerate the development of cities, states and countries. This strategy can be called eTransformation, and the Internet provides the connectivity essential for its success. Leaders with vision, consensus formation, public policies and institutions have central roles in an eTransformation strategy (Figure 2).

Figure 2: Simplified Links among Elements
of an eTransformation Strategy

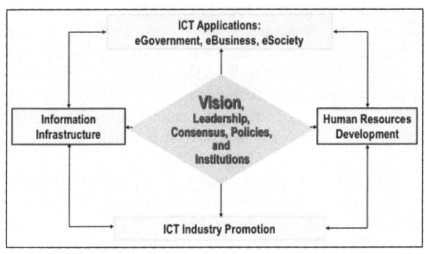

An eTransformation strategy cuts across economic sectors and government agencies, taking advantages of synergies and returns to scale in infrastructure – especially for broadband Internet connectivity, computing equipment, and software. Much of current development policy and practice treats elements of eTransformation in isolation, yet most of the documented failures of ICT applications in eGovernment, eBusiness, eEducation, and rural development are traced to fragmented approaches that missed key enablers, operated within separate bureaucratic domains, and ignored synergies between different sectors and scale economies to facilitate sustained transformation.[18]

Recent demonstrations in Brazil against corruption, impunity, and poor public services have highlighted institutional weaknesses. These weaknesses not only affect living standards, but also increase costs, reduce productivity and lower economic potential. All of these problems can be attacked using the powerful tools made available by the ICT revolution. Brazil's new transparency law that became effective for the federal, state, and municipal governments in May 2013 can be better implemented and corruption curtailed if information on government transactions, budget detail and execution of infrastructure projects are available online through transparency portals.

Improving the quality and reducing costs of education and health services, mapping crime in real time and deploying police forces more efficiently, easing traffic flow, and dealing with major emergencies through ICT-powered government operations centers are just a few of the ways in which information technology can strengthen the performance of institutions. Citizen service centers like São Paulo's *Poupatempo* (Timesaver), Bahia's Citizen Service Centers (*Serviço de Atendimento ao Cidadao* – SAC), and similar centers in other states are first steps in this direction. They speed the issuing of personal documents and other services in "one-stop shops" at locations and times convenient to citizens. [19]

Technological and economic rationale for an eTransformation strategy[20]

What is the underlying logic of this strategy? The starting point is the dramatic and continuing fall in the cost of processing, transmitting and storing data, information, and knowledge. The best-known principle of this revolution is Moore's Law, proposed by the cofounder and former CEO of Intel, Gordon Moore. Moore's law posits that the number of transistors that can be placed in an integrated circuit chip doubles every two years, yielding a 50% reduction in the unit cost of processing data. There are similar principles captured by other "laws", such as Butter's Law – according to which the quantity of data that can pass through an optical fiber doubles every nine months, leading to a fall in the unit transmission cost of 50% in the same period.

A key factor to consider in elaborating an eTransformation strategy is huge economies of scale in Internet infrastructure. Economies of scale are derived from the presence of high fixed costs but low marginal costs for providing increasing amounts of the good or service. The average cost per unit sold falls as the number of units sold increases. The main channels of the Internet – the trunk lines or backbone – are fiber optic cables, both terrestrial and submarine, connected to optical equipment like routers and to the datacenters of the principal operators.

These scale economies are derived from the very low marginal cost of adding more fibers to a cable before it is purchased and installed and also the fact that the same fiber base can subsequently be made more effective by replacing the optical technology used. Some additional equipment is needed, but these are broadband amplifiers and transceivers that can deal with many different channels simultaneously. Such equipment can multiply the initial speeds of transmission by tenfold or more.[21] Thus there are opportunities for different operators or users to collaborate when investing in fiber or other facilities that provide more capacity than needed at low cost. This excess capacity can be leased to or traded with other operators in return for access to their own excess fiber.

This is a win-win proposition because the costs to each operator for fibers in a shared cable is lower than if that operator alone had to bear all the costs of investment for the capacity it needs. The more partners share the investment costs, the lower the unit costs per user. While it is not widely known, since telecommunications operators rarely reveal sharing agreements, operators commonly have arrangements between themselves, financed by transfer payments or in-kind exchanges, to take advantage of these economies of scale.

A second factor favoring an eTransformation strategy is the continuous and rapid fall in the prices for the transmission, storage, and processing of information. Internet connectivity is essential for an eTransformation strategy. In microeconomics one of the first principles economists learn is that when the price of a good or service falls that good or service will be substituted for similar ones the prices of which are rising, stable, or falling less quickly. The extent of the substitution will depend on the "price elasticity of demand" for the good or service in question, that is the percentage increase in demand divided by the percentage increase in price. If demand increases faster than the price falls, the price elasticity is said to be greater than one, meaning that a reduction in prices (or taxes on the service) could produce more rather than less revenue.

It is the rapid decline in the cost of ICT goods and services (hardware, software, telecommunications) and the consequent potential to displace similar conventional goods and services that underlies this microeconomic argument in favor of an eTransformation strategy. But ease and speed of substitution can be influenced by subjective, cultural, managerial, and institutional factors. This "friction" can slow the substitution process. An eTransformation strategy seeks to reduce or remove such friction through political leadership, financial incentives, and strategic communication policies.

Realizing the potential benefits of ICT depends on many interdependent factors as summarized in Figure 2. In this book the focus is on the telecommunications infrastructure of the Internet and in general IP networks – with a strong focus on fiber optic cables and other infrastructure (e.g. coaxial and copper cables, cell towers, transmitters, and satellites). These technologies are used to reach end users when fiber to the home, building, or curb/cabinet (known as FTTx) is not available or – as for mobile devices such as smartphones, tablets and laptops – appropriate. But note that wireless technologies (cellular telephony, microwave links, satellites, etc.) all depend on terrestrial fiber connections to the backbone of the Internet. And this backbone is composed of fiber optic cables, both terrestrial and submarine, with the necessary optical equipment, routers, and datacenters at key nodes.

Structure of the book

The rest of this book is organized as follows. Chapter 2 provides some background regarding the origins of the Internet in the United States, Europe, and Brazil. Chapter 3 looks more closely at the development of the Internet in Brazil as regards coverage, quality, and digital inclusion of the population. Chapter 4 examines why Internet connectivity and mobile telephony (voice, data, and video) services in Brazil cost so much for such low quality compared with other countries. Chapter 5 analyzes what is being done to improve these services, reduce their cost, and make them available to the as yet unserved (digitally excluded) population.

Chapter 6 reviews how Brazil is dealing with privacy issues, including those raised during the furor unleashed by Edward Snowden's revelations regarding electronic surveillance, and what may be called the "dark side" of the Internet – spam; phishing; other forms of fraud; viruses, worms and other malware; and cyber-warfare. Chapter 7 analyzes the Brazilian model of Internet governance, how it developed, and how it can serve as a model for other countries or the global Internet.

Finally, building on the analysis of the earlier chapters, Chapter 8 deals with the future of the Internet in Brazil, presenting some recommendations for priority measures to reduce costs, expand coverage, improve quality, and increase competition.

Chapter 1: The Strategic Importance of the Internet for Brazil's Development

1   Zweig, S. (1943).

2   IBOPE Inteligência (2013).

3   These estimates are presented at http://en.wikipedia.org/ wiki/List_of_countries_by_GDP_(nominal). Accessed 25 February 2014.

4   IBGE (2013), Tabela 7.6.7 and http://seriesestatisticas.ibge. gov.br/series.aspx?vcodigo=fed103. Accessed 25/02/2014.

5   These estimates are presented at http://en.wikipedia.org/ wiki/List_of_countries_by_income_equality. Accessed 25 February 2014.

6   Schwab, K. (2013), p. 15.

7   Conner (2012).

8   http://www.internetworldstats.com/stats.htm. Accessed 25 January 2014.

9   ICT refers to technologies that provide access to information through telecommunications. It is similar to Information Technology (IT), but focuses primarily on communication technologies. This includes the Internet, wireless networks, cell phones, and other communication mediums.

10   Schumpeter (1950).

11   http://mobithinking.com/mobile-marketing-tools/latest-mobile-stats/a#uniquesubscribers. Accessed 23/01/2014. Original source: International Telecommunications Union (ITU).

12   http://www.teleco.com.br/pais/fixo_mundo.asp (accessed 23/01/2014). Original source: ITU.

13   The lower number is an estimate by Ericsson, the higher by Wireless Intelligence, as reported in http://mobithinking. com/mobile-marketing-tools/latest-mobile-stats/ a#uniquesubscribers (accessed 23/01/2014).

14   http://www.gartner.com/newsroom/id/2665715. Accessed 14 February 2014.

15   Mundy, (2014).

16   Lunden, (2013)

17   http://www.cisco.com/en/US/solutions/collateral/ns341/ns525/ns537/ns705/ns827/white_paper_c11-481360_ns827_Networking_Solutions_White_Paper.html. Accessed 25/01/2014.

18   Hanna & Knight (2011 and 2012).

19   Knight & Annenberg, (2008).

20   This section draws on Knight (2008).

21   Michael Stanton via e-mail correspondence, 16 February 2014.

Chapter 2

The Origins and Institutions of the Internet in Brazil

The Internet was born in the United States as a network of networks some nine years before it emerged in Brazil. But the origins go back much further, both in the United States and Europe, and in Brazil.

Early Developments in the United States and Europe[1]

The first steps in the development of the Internet came from work done by researchers at the Massachusetts Institute of Technology (MIT) in the 1960s to develop packet-switched communication between computers. The concept of networked computers connected by packet routing rather than circuit switching was first developed by J.C.R. Licklider of MIT in August 1962.

The idea of packet switching is that a packet of data that includes both its origin and destination can be sent from one location to the other. Licklider was the first head of the computer research program at the United States Defense Advanced Research Projects Agency (DARPA, now ARPA). Leonard Kleinrock at MIT published the first paper on packet switching theory in July 1961 and the first book on this subject in 1964.[2]

Another Internet pioneer who independently came up with a similar idea was Paul Baran. He worked at the RAND Corporation in California on a study financed by the United States Air Force to develop a decentralized communication system that would allow the military to maintain command and control of aircraft and nuclear missiles during and after a nuclear attack. This led to a series of papers titled "On Distributed Communications" that in 1964 described a detailed architecture for a distributed survivable packet-switched communications network.[3]

Vinton Cerf, one of the "fathers of the Internet" and today Vice President and Chief Internet Evangelist of Google explains Baran's role as follows:

> "Baran articulated the utility of packetization for voice although he called the units 'message blocks'. His system was never built, but his work became known to the ARPANET designers after the basic design work was done. While I was running the Internet program I wanted to make the Internet resilient to nuclear attack and even demonstrated its self-healing capability, using airborne packet radios, in cooperation with the Strategic Air Command. So Baran's ideas did find fertile ground in the Internet if not in the ARPANET." [4]

Packet switching provides greater security, maximum use of available bandwidth, communication between devices at different speeds, and resilience to line failure by diverting signals via the best routes at any instant in time so that communication can take place during disasters when telephone service is interrupted. Packet switching enabled creation of the research network ARPANET at the U.S. Defense Department. ARPANET became operational in 1969, when four host computers were connected, a first step in the building of the Internet. ARPANET was not designed for military use, as is commonly thought, but rather to support computer resource sharing among research universities backed by the Pentagon. In 1972, electronic mail, the first "killer application" was introduced.

The next critical advance was the invention of TCP/IP (Transmission Control Protocol/Internet Protocol) in 1973 and reported in a paper by Cerf and Robert Kahn in 1974. These protocols allowed what is known as "open architecture networking" permitting interconnection between diverse computer networks wherever located.[5] Further work for the Pentagon extended the concept to Packet Satellite and Packet Radio networks that were connected to the ARPANET in 1983, thereby launching the Internet.

Many other researchers contributed to the theory and design of what became ARPANET and then the Internet.[6]

As local area networks, microcomputers, and more advanced workstations became widely used in the 1980s, the Internet grew rapidly. In the mid-1980s ARPANET was linked to the academic NSFNET of the U.S. National Science Foundation. New Internet service providers began offering access to commercial customers. By 1995, it was supposed that academic users would no longer need dedicated networks, being adequately served by commercial ISPs, so the NSFNET was shut down. In 1996 a consortium called Internet2 launched a new academic and scientific network called Abilene as a private network run by the universities. Abilene operated at much higher speeds than those available over the commercial Internet.[7]

Meanwhile, another major breakthrough took place in Europe, at the European Organization for Nuclear Research (CERN), where Tim Berners-Lee invented a network-based implementation of the hypertext concept of links that became the World Wide

Web. Hypertext documents were expressed in Hypertext Markup Language (HTML), a basic code that facilitates access and communication on the Web. In 1993 the Web took off with the introduction of the first widely disseminated graphical web browser called Mosaic. Mosaic was developed by a team led by Marc Andreessen at the National Center for Supercomputing Applications, at the University of Illinois at Urbana-Champaign. The first mobile phone with Internet connectivity was the Nokia 9000 Communicator launched in Finland in 1996.

Gestation and Birth of the Brazilian Internet

The development of the Internet in Brazil began later. In 1975 the Ministry of Communications (MC) decided that Embratel, the long-distance carrier and part of the state-owned Telebras group, would be responsible for deploying, expanding and operating a National Telex Network and a National Data Transmission Network, including international connections.

That same year a connection with ARPANET was demonstrated by Vinton Cerf and Keith Uncapher at the First Latin American Seminar on Data Communication that took place during the Seventh National Conference on Data Processing in São Paulo, creating considerable excitement.[8]

In the late 1970s and early 1980s there was a growing interest in the convergence between telecommunications and computing or information science, sometimes called informatics (*informática* in Portuguese). This interest was reflected in major conferences and research programs in Brazil. In 1979, Telebras announced a project to create a Latin American Computer Network (*Rede Latina-Americana de Computadores* – REDLAC) with a view to developing research on packet switching, local area networks and the interconnection of networks. This research involved a group on data communication at the Telebras research center, CPqD, in Campinas (São Paulo state) in partnership with the University of São Paulo (USP). [9]

Protocol wars

During these years a clash emerged between the development of the TCP/IP-based communications, applied in increasingly open international partnerships, and the evolving industrial, technology, and import control policies of Brazil's nationalist military government. First elaborated in the Second National Development Plan during the administration of President Ernest Geisel and covering the years 1975-79, these industrial and technology policies sought to promote the development of a domestic industry for electronic components and inputs, technological autonomy (*vis à vis* other countries), and also a national equipment industry. These policies were developed as part of a second wave of import substitution, the first wave having begun during the Great Depression and continued during World War II and the 1950s.[10]

In the area of informatics, the principal institution charged with carrying out these policies was the Special Secretariat for Informatics (*Secretaria Especial de Informática* - SEI), created in 1979. It reported directly to the National Security Council of the government of President João Figueiredo (1979-1985). SEI was characterized by an authoritarian style and did not inspire confidence in the civilian technology community. SEI took control of the trans-border data flows (data crossing Brazil's frontiers). SEI supported a network architecture, Open Systems Interconnection (OSI), first published in draft by the International Organization of Standards (ISO) in 1981 and made an ISO standard in 1984, 11 years after the development of TCP/IP, a simpler and cheaper (its development was subsidized by the U.S. government) technology invented in the US. For the Brazilian military at that time, adoption of TCP/IP would "represent a reaffirmation of American hegemony."[11]

The policies implemented by SEI were aligned with a Third World movement that sought to create a New World Information and Communication Order, an offshoot of the New World Economic Order.[12] With the support and coordination of UNESCO, the Intergovernmental Bureau for Informatics was established in 1978 by 35 countries, including Brazil, and sought to promote informatics in developing countries, including legislation concerning trans-border data flows.

The Brazilian position was clearly articulated by Lt. General Joubert de Oliveira Brizida, Executive Secretary of SEI, during the First International Conference on Transborder Data Flows held in Rome, Italy in June 1980. "The country that does not concern itself with the control of strategic information that it uses runs the risk of becoming intolerably dependent, through telecommunications, on the interests of political and economic groups outside its frontiers."[13]

These movements and Brazil's informatics policies were generally antagonistic to the major developed countries, especially the United States, and the multinational companies originating in these countries. UNESCO's role in these movements was one of several factors leading the US, UK and Singapore to withdraw from UNESCO at the end of 1984. The nationalistic policies also made it difficult for Brazilian organizations (governmental, academic, civil society) and businesses to participate in the development of the Internet, since it relied on TCP/IP rather than OSI.

It should be added that some of the principal international corporations producing ICT equipment at that time (e.g. IBM, Burroughs, Digital Equipment Corporation) had their own proprietary technologies and this also was a factor holding back the adoption of TCP/IP.

But with the end of military rule in 1985, SEI was transferred from the National Security Council to the recently created Ministry of Science and Technology (MCT). Then at the beginning of the presidency of Fernando Collor, in 1990, SEI was disbanded and replaced by the Department of Informatics and Automation Policy (*Departamento de Política de Informática e Automatação* - DEPIN) in the Secretariat of Science and Technology, which replaced the MCT. DEPIN continued to control trans-border data flows in theory, but in practice with globalization and the growth of the Internet, it ceased to exercise its prerogatives.

The rise of the academic Internet

Meanwhile, in the academic community, there was growing interest in the formation of networks linking computers in different universities. The first moves in this direction took place in the southernmost Brazilian state, Rio Grande do Sul, where, in the mid-1970s, a project called the Southern Teleprocessing Network (*Rede Sul de Teleprocessamento* – RST) was launched, coordinated by Professor Liane Tarouco at the Federal University of Rio Grande do Sul (UFRGS). In 1973 she had met Professor Leonard Kleinrock, one of the ARPANET pioneers, who came to Brazil to teach a course on teleprocessing at the Catholic University of Rio de Janeiro (PUC-Rio). In 1977 Tarouco published the first book on data communication in Brazil. She then visited Stanford University and had practical contact with ARPANET. When she returned to UFRGS, Tarouco tried to establish a connection with ARPANET, but it proved too costly.[14]

The RST project never took off, but the interest in research on data communication networks in Brazilian universities did. At the end of 1979 the National Computer Network Laboratory (*Laboratório Nacional de Redes de Computadores* – LARC), a virtual entity to link institutions working in this area, was established. The Federal University of Rio de Janeiro (UFRJ) and PUC-Rio were especially active. In 1982 in PUC-Rio research began to develop a packet switch in a joint project with Telebras, Embratel, and USP called REDPUC. Specialized courses at PUC-Rio introduced hundreds of people to computer networking. In 1984 a project called Rio Network (*Rede Rio*), that would link computers in academic and research institutions in the city of Rio de Janeiro, was created, but it did not get off the ground, in part because financing from the Financing Agency for Studies and Projects (*Financiadora de Estudos e Projetos* - FINEP) ran out.

But interest in computer networking in Brazilian universities continued to grow, fueled by news of the creation of NSFNET in the US and parallel initiatives in other countries. By 1986 there were more than 50 academic networks in the world, but no Brazilian academic networks existed except on paper. There were, however a number of projects in discussion, mainly in São Paulo and Rio de Janeiro, to change this situation. These initiatives became better known in 1987, as the importance of academic networks for scientific research and exchange was recognized more widely by Brazilian academics.

After a so-called "birds of a feather" discussion of academic networking at the July 1986 congress of the Brazilian Computing Society, the National Council for Scientific and Technological Development (*Conselho Nacional de Desenvolvimento Científico e Tecnológico* – CNPq) made available funding for a three day meeting held that October at USP, organized by Professors Paulo Aguiar of UFRJ and Michael Stanton of PUC-Rio. This meeting, held at USP, brought together 38 academic researchers, representatives of the government (including SEI), and Embratel (the long-distance carrier of the state-owned Telebras group). They sought to develop a network to facilitate communication among Brazilian academic and scientific communities and with their colleagues in other countries."As a direct result of this meeting, the seed was sown for what would later develop into a purpose-built national research network. A final consequence was the Brazilian participation in the 6th International Networking Workshop, held the following month at Princeton, where for the first time extensive contacts were made with the international networking research community."[15]

In 1988 and 1989 three Brazilian institutions – the National Laboratory for Scientific Computing (LNCC) in Rio de Janeiro, the São Paulo Research Foundation (*Fundação de Amparo à Pesquisa do Estado de São Paulo* - FAPESP), and UFRJ – separately established network links with three different institutions in the United States using BITNET (Because It's Time Network), a network permitting the exchange of e-mails and files. These links had to be approved by Embratel and SEI, and this was achieved after a meeting in Brasília in April 1988. BITNET did not use the TCP/IP protocols, nor was a common connection between these three institutions and Bitnet possible given Brazilian legislation at that time.[16]

This legislation was initially circumvented by FAPESP treating all connected (state-run) institutions as part of a single legal entity. Thus the single ANSP (Academic Network at São Paulo) international link from FAPESP served the three state universities in São Paulo state -- USP, the State University of Campinas (Unicamp) and the State University of São Paulo (UNESP), among others. The LNCC link was also shared by granting remote terminal access for researchers to use the

BITNET-connected mainframe at LNCC in Rio de Janeiro. As the restrictions were relaxed, a mesh of network links spread out to other universities and laboratories throughout Brazil to form the Brazilian branch of BITNET, which operated until the mid-1990s. Figure 3 shows the extent of this network in 1991.[17]

Figure 3: RNP Leased Line BITNET Connections in December 1991

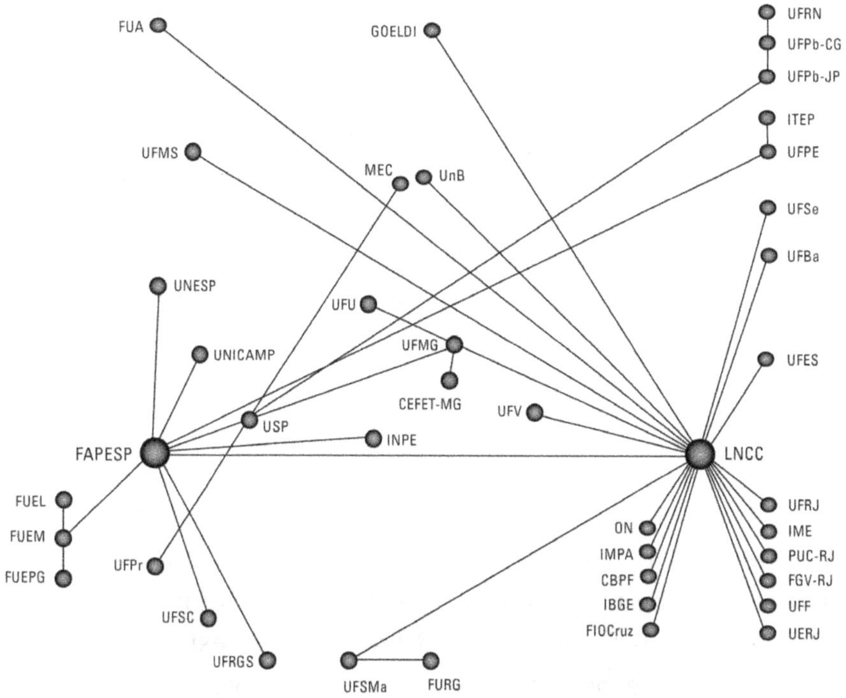

Source: Stanton (1993) p. GFB-8

The creation of a National Research Network (RNP), a broader and more ambitious project, required an extensive and expensive infrastructure that would depend on government resources. In mid-1988 a working group linked with the Chief of Staff of the Ministry of Science and Technology (MCT) was established, coordinated by Tadao Takahashi, then of the CNPq. Its work resulted in the decision of the MCT to support and finance the

RNP. In September 1989 RNP was launched during a conference in São Paulo. [18] It then began to operate a network of leased lines within Brazil in 1992 (Figure 4).

Takahashi, who became RNP's first coordinator, recruited Michael Stanton in mid-1990 as R&D coordinator. Together with Paulo Aguiar and Alexandre Grojsgold, Stanton was already planning a TCP/IP network to replace BITNET in Rio de Janeiro, where he had been appointed network coordinator of the Rio de Janeiro Research Foundation (*Fundação Carlos Chagas Filho de Amparo à Pesquisa do Estado do Rio de Janeiro* - FAPERJ) the previous year. By mid-1990 this project had progressed, and it began to be discussed within the Brazilian BITNET community. At first Takahashi did not favor using TCP/IP, but he was convinced to do so by Michael Stanton and Demi Getschko. Getschko was also recruited by Takahashi to coordinate the construction and operation of the future RNP. He was at that time in charge of IT operations at FAPESP, that had created the ANSP network in the BITNET era.[19]

Takahashi then launched a campaign to link the RNP with the Internet. But this resulted in a clash with SEI regarding the protocols to be used. SEI had tolerated the connections with BITNET. They did not use TCP/IP nor require establishment of a dedicated international link, "since there were still political barriers to the import of IP routers."[20]

Figure 4: RNP Network in 1992

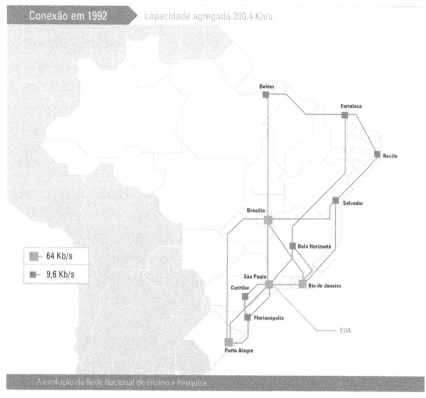

Source: RNP

In November 1990, a Brazilian workshop on High Performance Computing was held. Dr. Barry Leiner was an invited speaker at this workshop. He was a member of the Internet Activities Board, responsible for supervision of the Internet's operation and for international liaison. He was also a member of the Coordinating Committee for Intercontinental Research Networks. Leiner sought out some of the early academic networking organizers. They included Stanton (at that time coordinator, and presently Director of Research and Development of RNP), Paulo Aguiar of UFRJ and Demi Getschko of FAPESP, currently Chairman of the Executive Board of The Brazilian Network Information Center (NIC.br) and a member of CGI.br, as well as several other Brazilian network specialists.

In March of 1991, Getschko and Stanton traveled to the United States, representing the RNP, spending about three weeks participating in meetings of the Internet Engineering Task Force (IETF) and the United States Federal Engineering Planning Group and visiting various institutions involved in research, development, operation, and finance of research networks. A great deal was accomplished thanks to the intense planning prior to the trip by Tadao Takahashi (RNP) and Steve Goldstein (NSF).

For some time after its launch, the RNP made little progress in building its backbone. But also in1991, Ivan Moura Campos, who had academic and government experience, was named CNPq's Director of Special Programs. He became an important ally of the RNP, working behind the scenes to mobilize political and financial support. By the beginning of 1992, the first version of RNP's backbone became operational (Figure 4).

Brazil joined the global Internet in May 1992 with two international links set up by academic institutions during the United Nations Conference on Environment and Development (UNCED), better known as the Earth Summit or Eco 92, in Rio de Janeiro.

Civil society networks: Alternex

Meanwhile interest in networking was also growing in the Brazilian community of NGOs, led by the efforts of Carlos Afonso, currently President of the Brazilian chapter of the Internet Society and a member of CGI.br.[21] Afonso returned to Brazil after the 1979 amnesty for Brazilian exiles who had left Brazil during the most repressive years of the military dictatorship. Together with Herbert de Souza (better known as Betinho), he founded the Brazilian Institute for Social and Economic Analyses (*Instituto Brasileiro de Análises Sociais e Econômicas* – IBASE) in 1981 and became a tireless promoter of networking between NGOs, both in Brazil and around the world. He was also a successful mobilizer of financial support for his networking efforts and used his technical skills and connections in international organizations, foundations, and Brazilian government agencies to help build Alternex, beginning with a Bulletin Board System (BBS) in 1985 and then a network of Brazilian NGOs in 1987. He obtained support from the UNDP and NGOs in other countries, including the Institute for Global Communication (IGC) in the US. He was a co-funder of the Association for Progressive Computing (APC), a global network. Through Alternex he also established the first non-academic dialup link to the Internet in 1989 (between Alternex and IGC), managing to slip "under the radar" of SEI and Embratel.

Afonso sought allies in the academic networking community of Rio de Janeiro in mid-1990. IBASE, as representative of the APC in Brazil, prepared a detailed project to provide support to connections to the Internet during the UNCED. He then conducted arduous negotiations with the conference secretariat over more than a year with the support of the RNP, especially Tadao Takahashi, and sympathizers in UNDP, to get approval of the UNCED Information Strategy Project in Rio. That project was included in the formal agreement between UNCED and the Brazilian government establishing the framework for Eco-92.

With the approval of this project it was possible for Alternex to do a massive upgrade of its computers, allowing it to connect all the spaces of Eco-92, including the pressroom and the Global Forum (a parallel event for NGOs that attracted almost 9,000 NGOs from around the world), to the Internet. These connections were facilitated by the provision of IP addresses from Rio de Janeiro's brand new academic network, *Rede Rio*. That network was supported by FAPERJ, the president of which at that time was

Fernando Peregrino. Alternex also gave some of the equipment it received to the RNP.

Embratel dragged its feet in providing international connectivity, but could not avoid providing the links that the Brazilian government had guaranteed to the United Nations. The UNCED operation that launched the Brazilian Internet thus involved an effective partnership between Brazilian academic, government, and civil society organizations and international bodies, including the United Nations system, NGOs (especially APC), and foundations.

After the event, Alternex continued its collaboration with *Rede Rio* and became the first Brazilian ISP. Its use of *Rede Rio* resulted in polemics, since Alternex charged some of its customers to cover its costs, but used *Rede Rio's* connectivity to the Internet free of charge. This "commercial" activity was seen by some of *Rede Rio's* leaders as contrary to the purposes of an academic network. In 1992, even before the Earth Summit, Alternex had started the first program to help BBSs become ISPs.More than 150 BBSs eventually made the transition with the support of Alternex. But eventually this activity aggravated the disagreement with key leaders of *Rede Rio*. This resulted in *Rede Rio* cutting Alternex's link to the Internet. Nevertheless, RNP continued to provide Internet access for Alternex from its Rio PoP (Point of Presence) using FAPESP's international link. IBASE sought to encourage new Internet entrepreneurs, but did not seek privatization of the Telebras system.

First steps of the commercial Internet and the birth of CGI.br

With the invention of the World Wide Web in 1989 at the European Organization for Nuclear Research (CERN) in Geneva and easy-to-use browsers (beginning with Mosaic in 1992 and Netscape, launched in 1994), the growth of the Internet accelerated throughout the world. What had been essentially an academic and research network, also used by some large organizations and technology enthusiasts, was increasingly in demand for commercial activity. What were previously complex operations requiring specialized knowledge for anything beyond e-mail, became easy to undertake with a simple click of a mouse, catalyzing a huge increase in Internet traffic and a surge of entrepreneurial activity that were mutually reinforcing.

Commercial use of the Internet in Brazil only began in 1995, the year NSFNET was decommissioned, after a pilot trial by Embratel in December 1994. When Embratel began its commercial service, a fear arose in the growing Brazilian Internet community that Embratel would monopolize the Brazilian commercial Internet.

President Fernando Henrique Cardoso, who took office on 1 January 1995, was determined to end the state monopoly in telecommunications. In this endeavor, he had strong support from his Minister of Communications, Sérgio Motta. Motta determined in April 1995, through Norm No 004-1995, that Internet access was a value-added service over which there would be no monopoly. Norm 004-1995 defined "Internet Connection Service" as a "generic name that designates a value-added service that allows access to the Internet by users and providers of information services." Motta then announced that Embratel would have to cease providing access to physical persons and rejected Embratel's attempt to charge a special rate for Internet users. That assured that emerging small ISPs like those incubated by IBASE would be free to grow.

Norm 4 thus resulted in one of the defining characteristics of Internet service provision in Brazil not observed in most other countries – the emergence of thousands of small and medium

ISPs that serve remote areas or poorer markets where the large incumbent telcos and newer large-scale operators have yet to seek customers. Indeed, as will be seen in Chapter 3, many of these small and medium local ISPs compete successfully with the large operators by providing better quality service both technically and because they have an intimate knowledge of their customers.

It took three years to enact the needed legislation that privatized the state-run telecoms. Meanwhile conditions had to be created for the commercial Internet to grow outside the control of the soon-to-be-extinct state-run telecoms. The new ISPs obtained access to the Internet either from state-run Embratel or from RNP, until the newly privatized telecoms took over in the late 1990s.

To monitor developments, and to draw up new rules for the Internet in Brazil, the Brazilian Internet Steering Committee (CGI. br) was created by Inter-ministerial (MCT and MC) Ordinance 147, of 31 May 1995, later amended by Presidential Decree 4,829 of 3 September 2003. CGI.br's mandate is to coordinate and integrate all Internet service initiatives in Brazil, as well as promote technical quality, innovation, and the dissemination of the services available. CGI.br supported the newly created Brazilian commercial Internet through public-private cooperation. CGI's role will be explored in some detail in Chapter 7 that focuses on the Brazilian model of Internet governance.

The same Inter-Ministerial Ordinance allowed commercial ISPs to connect to RNP. This ordinance was the result of extensive political maneuvering behind the scenes on the part of Ivan Moura Campos in the MCT; Renato Guerreiro, then Secretary of Communications in the MC; and IBASE's leader, Betinho, working in close coordination with Carlos Afonso of Alternex.

Brazil's telecommunications law, privatization, institutions, and market structure

The current institutional framework of Brazil's telecommunications system was established by Law 9472 of 16 July 1997, the General Telecommunications Law (*Lei Geral de Telecomunicações* – LGT). This law created the National Telecommunications Agency (Anatel) as the regulatory agency charged with defending the interests of the State and the citizen, encouraging competition, universalizing telecommunications services, and updating telecommunications technology.

The LGT, together with Constitutional Amendment nº 8 of 15 October 1995, ended the state monopoly under Telebras, the holding company that controlled public-sector telecoms in each state until their privatization in 1998. The goal of the privatization was to create a competitive telecommunications market and provide a wider range of affordable telecommunications to Brazil's population. Three regional telcos emerged from the privatization: Telefônica in São Paulo, the largest market, Telemar (now called Oi) in the northern, northeastern and southeastern states, and Brazil Telecom in the center-west, west, and south of the country. All of them but Telemar were controlled by foreign telcos.

In 2008 Brasil Telecom was absorbed by Oi (that in March 2014 was being merged with Portugal Telecom), reducing the incumbent regional telcos to two. Embratel continued as a long-distance operator, but has moved into mobile telephony (Claro) and cable TV (Net), all controlled by Telmex, a Mexican company. Today all of them offer Internet access, having formed subsidiaries for this purpose.

In 1999 in each region and for Embratel's national coverage for long-distance and international calls, a second new operator, called a "mirror" (*empresa espelho*) was created by open auctions, establishing duopolies, though the new entrants had to start virtually from scratch to build their networks, and were thus at a considerable disadvantage, though they could take advantage of up-to-date technologies. In 2002 the mirror companies in each region had only 1% of the traffic.[22]

Beginning in 2002 there were no restrictions on the number of new entrants, so soon there were also "little mirrors" (*espelhinhos*). Two mirrors for Embratel, Vesper and Intelig, were bought out by Embratel in 2003, and TIM in 2009 respectively. The largest original mirror, initially in the Brasil Telecom region, Global Village Telecom (GVT), has been very successful in expanding its fiber optic network and is now active in 20 states, offering high-speed broadband and other services. GVT was bought by the French company Vivendi in 2009.

There is considerable competition between the four major mobile providers (Oi, TIM, Vivo, and Claro), and in some states smaller operators. But for fixed-line telephone and internet service the regional incumbents, Vivo/Telefônica and Oi, enjoyed near monopolies in their regions for some years, having extensive fiber and microwave backbones and last mile copper networks in the richest markets.

Like incumbents in the United States and many other countries, they find ways to resist "unbundling", to maintain market share, despite legal obligations to do so. Unbundling means the duty to provide, to any requesting telecommunications carrier, for the provision of a telecommunications service, nondiscriminatory access to network elements at any technically feasible point on rates, terms, and conditions that are just, reasonable, and nondiscriminatory. Examples include leasing access to their last-mile and backbone fiber networks, making wholesale sales of bandwidth, and leasing dark fiber to competitors both large and small.

Anatel has administrative independence and financial autonomy while officially linked to the Ministry of Communications. Anatel's directors are appointed by the President of the Republic for fixed terms after approval by the Federal Senate. The LGT already foresaw the need for unbundling. Then came rules for requiring wholesale sales of bandwidth based on costs. But Anatel has been too weak to enforce its own regulations.

One of the reasons for Anatel's weakness is that its funding has been cut way below what was originally envisaged. This funding comes from the federal budget and the Telecommunications Supervision Fund (*Fundo de Fiscalização das Telecomunicações* - Fistel). Fistel's revenues come from a variety of sources, the most important being fees for maintaining phone numbers. Fiscal revenue for the period 2001-2012 totaled R$44.2 billion, but Anatel has received only about 10% of this revenue.[23] Another reason for Anatel's weakness is pressure brought to bear on Anatel and the Ministry of Communications by the powerful incumbents.

To finance coverage for remote and poorer markets, in 2000 the Fund for the Universalization of Telecommunications Services (*Fundo de Universalização dos Serviços de Telecomunicações* - Fust) was established, as provided for in the LGT. Fust is financed mainly by a 1% tax on the gross revenue of telecommunications operators and part of Fistel revenues. Over the period 2001-2012 Fust revenue totaled R$14.3 billion, of which R$1.9 billion was collected in 2012.[24] It was simply not used for its intended purpose.

Likewise, the Fund for Development of Telecommunications Technologies (*Fundo para o Desenvolvimento de Tecnológico das Telecomunicações* - Funttel), that receives 0.5% of all telecommunications bills, has used only 40 to 50% of its revenues for this purpose.

Instead, the Ministry of Finance has diverted virtually all of the Fust 90% of Fistel, and 50 to 60% of Funttel revenues to help build a primary surplus to pay interest on the federal debt. Legislation to change the destination of Fust resources has languished in Congress since 2007, as will be further discussed in Chapter 5.

Chapter 2: Origins and Institutions of the Internet in Brazil

1   A long list of sources on Internet history with links to each can be found on the site of the Internet Society, http://www.internetsociety.org/internet/what-internet/history-internet. Accessed 27 January 2014. Particularly useful is Leiner, et al. (1996). See also Haffner & Lyon (1996), a book written in journalistic style and Slater, (2002), a presentation with detailed information on a long list of Internet pioneers.

2   Kleinrock (1961) and (1964).

3   Baran (1964)

4   E-mail communications, October 2013.

5   Open architecture networking is described as follows in Leiner et al. (1996), p. 3 "In this approach, the choice of any individual network technology was not dictated by a particular network architecture but rather could be selected freely by a provider and made to interwork with the other networks through a meta-level "Internetworking Architecture". Up until that time there was only one general method for federating networks. This was the traditional circuit switching method where networks would interconnect at the circuit level, passing individual bits on a synchronous basis along a portion of an end-to-end circuit between a pair of end locations."

6   See Slater (2002) for biographical notes on a long list of Internet pioneers.

7   http://en.wikipedia.org/wiki/Abilene_Network.

8   Menezes de Carvalho (2006), p. 55.

9   Ibid. p. 56.

10   See Baer (2001), especially chapters 4-6, and Dantas (1988).

11   E-mail correspondence with Luiz Oscar Dantas, 28 January 2014.

12 See articles in Wikipedia: http://en.wikipedia.org/wiki/New_World_Information_and_Communication_Order and http://en.wikipedia.org/wiki/New_International_Economic_Order Both accessed 27 January 2014.

13 Dantas (1988) p 144.

14 Menezes de Carvalho (2006), p. 74.

15 Stanton (1993), p. CFB-3.

16 Menezes de Carvalho (2006), p. 84.

17 Correspondence with Michael Stanton, 16 February 2014.

18 Menezes de Carvalho (2006), p. 89.

19 Correspondence with Michael Stanton, 16 February 201.

20 Menezes de Carvalho (2006), p. 90.

21 The following paragraphs draw heavily on Menezes de Carvalho (2006) pp 111-120, Peregrino & Porto (2004) and a CV of Carlos Afonso at http://www.cgi.br/eleicao2010/cvs/CarlosAfonso.pdf. Accessed 28 January 2014.

22 Considera et al., p. 8

23 In 2012, for example, Fistel revenue totaled R$4.9 billion, while Anatel's actual expenditures totaled R$364 million, and authorized expenditures unpaid at the end of the year were R$79 million. Anatel (2013), pp. 115 and 117.

24 Anatel (2013), p. 116 and Anatel (2012), p. 19.

Chapter 3

Development of the Internet in Brazil

How has the Brazilian Internet grown? How is it being used? What are some of the principal problems it faces? These are some of the questions to be addressed in this chapter.[1]

Fixed and mobile Internet use

Detailed statistics on the Internet in Brazil and its use by individuals, households and businesses have been collected by the CGI.br's research arm, the Center for Studies on Information and Communication Technologies (*Centro de Estudos sobre as Tecnologias da Informação e da Comunicação* - CETIC.br), and also in less detail by the Brazilian Institute of Geography and Statistics (*Instituto Brasileiro de Geografia e Estatística* - IBGE) through its National Household Sample Survey (*Pesquisa Nacional por Amostra de Domicílios* - PNAD), both since 2005.[2]

According to the latest PNAD, published in 2013, 83 million persons 10 years of age or older accessed the Internet in the three months prior to the survey in 2012. The CETIC.br surveys show that the percentage of Brazil's population aged 10 or over that accessed the Internet during the three months prior to the survey rose from 30% in 2005 to 49% in 2012 (the latest year for which statistics are available) and homes with Internet access increased from 21% to 40%. The percentage of businesses with 10 or more employees that accessed the Internet in the last 12 months was virtually stable, 96% in 2005 and 97% in 2012, but the sample of businesses had more than tripled in size. Of those businesses with Internet access, the percentage having a website fell slightly from 59% to 55%.

Table 1: Percentage of Individuals Who Accessed the Internet, 2012

C2 - PROPORÇÃO DE INDIVÍDUOS QUE ACESSARAM A INTERNET - ÚLTIMO ACESSO
C2 - PROPORTION OF INDIVIDUALS WHO HAVE ACCESSED THE INTERNET BY LAST ACCESS
Percentual sobre o total da população[1]
Percentage of the total population[1]

Percentual (%) / Percentage (%)			Há menos de 3 meses (usuário)[2] - Less than three months ago (user)[2]
TOTAL			49
Área /	Area	**Urbana /** Urban	54
		Rural / Rural	18
Região /	Region	**Sudeste /** Southeast	55
		Nordeste / Northeast	38
		Sul / South	53
		Norte / North	36
		Centro-Oeste / Center-West	53
Sexo /	Sex	**Masculino /** Male	47
		Feminino / Female	50
Grau de instrução /	Level of education	**Analfabeto / Educação infantil / Iliterate / Pre-school**	1
		Fundamental / Elementary	30
		Médio / Secondary	72
		Superior / Tertiary	93
Faixa etária /	Age group	**De 10 a 15 anos /** 10 to 15 years old	70
		De 16 a 24 anos / 16 to 24 years old	74
		De 25 a 34 anos / 25 to 34 years old	62
		De 35 a 44 anos / 35 to 44 years old	46
		De 45 a 59 anos / 45 to 59 years old	31
		60 anos ou mais / 60 years or older	0
Renda familiar /	Family income	**Até 1 SM /** Up to 1 MW	18
		Mais de 1 SM até 2 SM / More than 1 and up tp 2 MW	33
		Mais de 2 SM até 3 SM / More than 2 and up to 3 MW	51
		Mais de 3 SM até 5 SM / More than 3 and up to 5 MW	69
		Mais de 5 SM até 10 SM / More than 5 and up tp 10	82
		Mais de 10 SM / More than 109 MW	91
Classe social /	Social class	**A**	94
		B	80
		C	47
		DE	14
Condição de atividade /	Economic activity status	**PEA /** Economically active population	52
		Não PEA / Economically inactive population	43

[1] Base: 166.605.600 pessoas. Respostas estimuladas. Dados coletados entre outubro de 2012 e fevereiro de 2013.
[1] Base: 166 600 000 persons. Stimulated answers. Data collected between October 2012 and February 2013.
[2] Considera-se "usuário" aquele que utilizou o computador há menos de três meses em relação ao momento da entrevista.
[2] A "user" is an individual who the Internet less than the three months prior to the interview.

Source: CETIC.br (2013), Table C2.

Looking now at the homes with a computer (46% of all homes in 2012), in 2012 40% had some kind of Internet access, up from only 13% in 2005. Interestingly, of the 24.3 million residences with Internet access, in 2012, only 7% relied on dialup service, while 67% had some kind of fixed broadband connection (cable, telephone line [DSL], radio, or satellite). Another 21% had mobile broadband (3G modem, but excluding smartphones). Differentials by region, income, and socio-economic class followed the same pattern seen in individual access.

In short, digital inclusion of individuals and households has advanced substantially, but much remains to be done to reach the poorer regions and individuals, older population groups, and rural areas.

Fixed broadband connections at the end of 2013 totaled 22.3 million, up 11% over the year, providing about 39% of Brazilian homes with this kind of connectivity.[3] Fixed broadband is available in all 5570 municipalities, at least in the municipal seats (municipalities include smaller towns and considerable rural areas, especially in the more sparsely populated parts of Brazil). Thanks to this availability, 66,000 urban public elementary and middle schools received free broadband connections under the Broadband in the Schools program.[4] This program was initiated in April 2008, when the telcos assumed this obligation in place of the requirement to establish "telecommunications service posts" in every municipal seat, as explained further in Chapter 5.

Third generation (3G) wireless broadband coverage has been growing fast, covering 3,564 or 64% of Brazil's municipalities with some 91% of Brazil's population as of December 2013.[5] The number of wireless broadband connections had reached 103.1 million, an astonishing increase of 74% in only one year.

Of these connections, 94.8 million were to cellphones, including smartphones, and 7 million to data terminals (including modems and tablets, but excluding debit and credit card readers). In addition there were 1.3 million new, much faster 4G mobile connections.[6]

The rapid increase in smartphone and tablet penetration should lead to a strong demand for fourth generation (4G) Long Term Evolution (LTE) mobile service with speeds on the order of 10 times those offered by 3G technologies like HSPA+ (offered by Vivo and Claro with speeds of 3 and 6 Mbps). As of 29 January 2014 LTE service was available from Vivo, Claro, TIM and/or Oi in 98 municipalities, including the capitals of 23 of Brazil's 26 states and the Federal District. Together these municipalities have 35.9% of Brazil's population. The service is available in all 12 World Cup cities.[7]

Brazil's mobile broadband penetration rate of 35 per 100 inhabitants at the end of 2013[8] was slightly higher than for Portugal, but about 37% of that in the United States.[9] In the third quarter of 2013 alone smartphone sales reached 10.4 million, 147% of sales in the same period of 2012. In January 2104 unblocked Android smartphones were selling for as low as US$ 88 in Brazilian online stores. Smartphones sold by mobile operators with a contract are cheaper than unblocked ones, many of which can use SIMs (Subscriber Identity Module – a small removable plastic card that identifies the company and carrier in a mobile phone) from more than one operator.

In recent years, CETIC.br has done studies on specific uses of the Internet: in education, health, non-profit organizations, ISPs, for youths 9-16 years old, and for children 5-9 years old.

These surveys provide a wealth of information, with many tables available online.[10]

As an example, consider some data on educational uses of the Internet. 91% of students in the 9th through the 11th year of school accessed the Internet in the three months prior to the survey. Students made extensive use of the Internet to for a wide variety of educational purposes, the most common being doing research for school (86%), projects (76%), group exercises (72%), and exercises required by their teacher (63). Percentages are consistently higher for private as compared with public schools.

Social networks are very popular. Brazil is the second largest market in the world for Facebook, exceeded only by the United States. Brazil had 67.9 million accounts as of March 2013, up by 79% in a year, making it an increasingly powerful communication tool. Of these the heaviest users were in the 18-24 age group, with male and female users both more than 10 million. The second biggest group was those aged 25-34, with female users about 10 million, and males about 8 million.[11] Twitter has more than 14 million users, third after the United States and Japan.[12] In July 2013 Brazil had some 14 million LinkedIn users, again the second largest in the world, exceeded only by the United States.[13]

YouTube had 38.9 million unique views in 2013, or 84 per viewer. Brazilian internauts in December 2012 spent an average of 9.3 hours on social media sites, or 77% more than the world average, out of a total 27 hours online. The fastest growing category of Brazilians' Internet use was politics. It grew 189% during the year 2012, but that was still only 19% of the time spent on beauty/fashion/style. [14]

The role of small Internet pioneers in digital inclusion[15]

The rapid expansion of Internet use is changing living standards even in the remote areas of Brazil. In 1986 Adilson Klaffke's family arrived in the region of Nova Guarita, now a town of 2,500 people in the far north of Mato Grosso that developed in the 1980s as a result of the gold rush in the deforested fringes of Brazil's Amazon region. The family came from São Miguel do Oeste in Santa Catarina, started farming and then diversified into selling lumber. But their son Adilson, now 38 years old, took another course, becoming a technician fixing television sets, and later teaching himself to be an IT professional, selling and repairing computers. Six years ago he leased a small dedicated link of 1 megabit per second (Mbps) from the telephone company Oi. This link ran from Sinop, called the Capital of the Far North, a city of 110,000 inhabitants about 200 kilometers to the southwest to Nova Guarita. Adilson launched an Internet service provider, Lasernet, that served 320 users in the town and seven *agrovilas* (clusters of housing within agricultural settlements) in the vicinity.

"I provide better quality service than Oi", says Adilson. "With this I can win clients in the *agrovilas*." Even the Transportation Department (Detran) in the town uses my service. Previously, Detran would not issue documents because it had no access to the Internet." Now the farmers use their connections to order agricultural inputs and to access technical information, weather forecasts, news of Brazil and the world and to maintain contact with relatives and friends in the South of Brazil.

In 2013, Klaffke got approval for a Multimedia Communication Service (*Serviço de Comunicação Multimídia* - SCM) license from Anatel. This license allows him to offer not only broadband, but also telephone and cable TV services. For others, obtaining a SCM license is too expensive. Many providers could pay the license fee (recently lowered to R$ 400, about US$170), but they cannot meet all the requirements set by Anatel, such as hiring a telecommunications engineer. The result is a high degree of informality. According to the estimates of the Brazilian Association of Internet and Telecommunications Providers (*Associação Brasileira de Provedores de Internet e Telecomunicações* - Abrint), there are about 9,000 providers, both licensed and informal, operating in thousands of municipalities all over Brazil.

The history of development in Brazil's interior is intrinsically related to the expansion of the means of communication. In the Amazon state of Rondônia, the installation of a telegraph line, in 1909, and the opening of a highway, BR-364, along the path of the telegraph line promoted the region's development and the birth of Cacoal, in Rondônia, a municipality that now has fiber optic cables.

With a population of about 80,000, Cacoal is served by Speed Travel, a small Internet service provider (ISP) run by 30 year-old Ed Carlo Saboia. Born in Rondonópolis, Mato Grosso, the son of parents who migrated from Ceará in the Northeast, Saboia began to work at a local local ISP in 2000 after the family moved to Rondônia. The firm's owner sold out to Saboia and his father in 2003. Young Saboia rapidly grew the business. Today Speed Travel has 10 employees and 3,500 customers. He built a 40-kilometer fiber optic ring that serves not only Cacoal, but also the neighboring municipalities of Pimenta Buena and Vilhena.

José Selestino started his Internet business in the small town of Uruará in Pará, astride the Transamazon highway, a continental road still unpaved and plagued by mud and potholes. Four years ago, this 33 year-old broadband trailblazer leased a fiber optic link originating in Brasília, built towers, installed Wi-Fi equipment, and provided technical support to maintain the loyalty of his clients.

Speed has been critical in the competitive market of small and medium ISPs. The viability of the business depends on creating customer loyalty. Customer loyalty depends on faster and more efficient connections. The career of Leandro Dias de Almeida, owner of Direct WiFi, in Campo Magro, Paraná, reflects the effort made by many young entrepreneurs all over Brazil. The business started small. Direct Wi-Fi leased a 1 Mbps radio link with which Almeida served 15 customers. In 2011 the business doubled: he leased a 2 Mbps link from Copel, the state electric power company, and the clientele reached 30. The next year, the business doubled in size again, with a 4 Mbps link. Up until then the growth had been merely geometric. He made a great leap in 2013, by leasing a fiber link of 200 Mbps. Like Saboia in Rondônia, speed was Dias de Almeida's business.

There are many other young Internet entrepreneurs all over Brazil: for example, Samuel Pereira and Asafe Coimbra of NetRocinha in Rio; Renato Salomão de Oliveira of Rondonet, with its headquarters in Ariquimes, Rondônia; and Roberto Filgueiras of Print Internet, in Macaé, Rio de Janeiro. Brazil has some 4,000 small ISPs registered with Anatel.

Brazil's myriad of small service providers is a rarity in the global Internet economy. In most countries Internet services are offered only by a few large companies, many of them government monopolies. "Some countries have no independent provider," says Basílio Perez, president of Abrint. "The diversity in Brazil should be encouraged." Many small providers began as dialup operations around 1995. "Since many of them have 18 years of experience", says Perez, "we can say that this market is reaching maturity."

The small providers are mostly in small towns. In big cities the market is dominated by big companies, mainly the incumbent telcos created at the time of privatization (Oi that merged with Brasil Telecom in 2008, Telefonica, and Embratel). There are an increasing number of insurgent providers of fiber connections entering the market (e.g. GVT, Cemig Telecom, Copel Telecom, and TIM). Initially the service was offered by telephone companies using existing infrastructure, as with Telefônica's Speedy and Oi's Velox.

Later, cable TV companies like Net (controlled by Embratel) entered, expanding the market for broadband and competing with the regional telcos and some new operators. Until recently, cable TV companies shunned small cities where the population density and income levels discouraged investments. Their absence provided opportunities for small entrepreneurs, who began operating via wireless links – at lower costs and prices – and then, as they grew and acquired financial capacity, switched to optical fiber. When these providers get an SCM license, they can add subscription TV services. The channels are usually received by a satellite ground station, then injected into the provider's fiber network. With small differences, this is the story of Kalffke, Saboia, Dias de Almeida and many other small providers.

Small entrepreneurs like those in Brazil's Amazon region are important, linking national trunk lines to remote places, as if moved by the "invisible hand of the market" described well over two centuries ago by Adam Smith in *The Wealth of Nations*. "It is not from the benevolence of the butcher, the brewer, or the baker, that we expect our dinner, but from their regard to their own interest," Smith wrote.[16]

Youth, political participation and the Internet

Today almost all young people have access to the Internet and, as demonstrated above, are extremely active on social media. Their devices may not have all the latest capabilities, but access, even when precarious, is widely available.

While researching for this book, I met young people from the periphery of São Paulo who were participating in the Reading Circles Program of the Fernand Braudel Institute that has reached thousands of students in public schools in low-income suburbs of Greater São Paulo and in states of the Northeast. I asked these youths how they used the Internet. They all said that they used broadband daily, almost all in their own homes. One uses a Wi-Fi connection of a neighbor (for which he paid about R$15 [US$6] per month). Many also accessed the Internet from smartphones and sometimes from lanhouses (paid public access points usually operated by young entrepreneurs), where many had their first contact with the Internet. All are connected with friends through Facebook and sometimes by e-mail, which is used for more formal communications. They download music, watch films in streaming video, research using Google and seek knowledge – and not only for their school work.

"I have the Internet in my DNA," said Mateus Gomes Sousa Santos, an eighth-grade student from a municipal school in São Miguel Paulista. "If I don't have access to the Internet I feel isolated and stressed. The Internet is a basic and essential service in all homes," said Bhrian Machado da Silva. "Today, someone who has no access at home can get it anywhere, like a lanhouse, a library, a community center, or at work. The Internet is a necessity, not only to communicate, but to learn, meet people, and locate old friends," said Mariana Silva da França. "In our school, the teacher helps us to prepare for technical courses that complement our middle school. He poses questions, then we search for the answers on the Internet and send them to him by e-mail. And then we discuss the results face to face," says Luis Guilherme Castro.

The Internet has become an instrument for political mobilization and more direct and continuous participation through social media. It can not easily be controlled by governments.[17] Young people like those in the Braudel Institute Reading Circles participated in the demonstrations that began in June 2013 throughout Brazil. The demonstrations were initially catalyzed by an overdue increase in bus fares to adjust for increases in the cost of bus service. But they then deepened and broadened to include such matters as corruption; impunity of politicians and others who have committed crimes; and underinvestment in education, health, public safety, and infrastructure.

All the demonstrations have been organized and monitored via social media over the Internet and using mobile phones. A poll of demonstrators in the capitals of seven Brazilian states conducted by the Brazilian equivalent of Gallup (IBOPE) found that 78% of participants in the protests learned about them via social media, and 75% used social media to invite friends to join them.[18] Participants in the demonstrations used photographs and video posted to Facebook and Twitter, etc. to report directly to each other and the world, bypassing the traditional print and electronic media that they have accused of biased and inaccurate reporting.

Interestingly, among the BRICS countries (Brazil, Russia, India, China and South Africa), Brazil has the largest percentage of "digital natives", defined as individuals in the 15-24 age group who have used the Internet for at least five years, both as a percent of the total population and as a percent of this age group.

Brazil's rank by both these measures is also above Argentina and Mexico, but far below South Korea (Table 2).[19]

Table 2: Digital Natives in Selected Countries, 2012

Country	Digital Natives (millions)	DN as % of Pop	DN as % of Youth	Youth as % of Pop	DN as % of Pop (Rank)
Brazil	20.1	10.1	60.2	16.8	37
Russia	9.0	6.3	49.6	12.7	84
India	22.7	1.8	9.5	18.9	139
China	75.2	5.6	34.7	16.0	89
S. Africa	1.8	3.6	18.6	19.6	111
Argentina	3.6	8.6	52.5	16.5	53
Mexico	9.1	7.8	43.3	18.1	66
S. Korea	6.6	13.5	99.6	13.5	3

Source: ITU (2013), Table 2.2, p. 143

A majority of protesters of this "Brazilian Fall" were probably digital natives, given their methods of organization and communication. They have emulated and further developed the techniques used by Tunisian, Egyptian, Syrian, and Turkish protesters of the "Arab Spring", the "Occupy" movement in the United States, the *Indignadas* in Spain, and the "Kitchenware Revolution" in Iceland.[20] In Brazil as in the United States, this movement reflects the low and decreasing legitimacy of representative democracy where citizen participation is mediated by political parties and limited to periodic voting.[21]

Citizens increasingly perceive legislators and political parties as having been bought by well-financed lobbies and corporate interests, resulting in further disillusionment of citizens with political institutions. This perception is strongest among younger generations, composed of the above-mentioned digital natives. They are accustomed to rapid communication and transactions over the Internet facilitated by the rapid growth of social media. But almost spontaneous outbursts of activity of the kind discussed above may not be enough to promote systemic reform in the short run, as appears to have been the fate of the Occupy movement in the United States.

Well-coordinated movements guided through social media Internet can bring down governments (as in Tunisia and Egypt). And there is a great potential to use the Internet and social media to structure to promote broad and deep debates on public policies, sometimes with the intermediation of civil society organizations and/or the traditional media as has been happening in Brazil. What is necessary to get results in a democratic framework is probably getting agreement on a set of specific demands that can be met in the short run (one set of demands) and the medium run (a second set) with continued pressure to get them met.

The most successful movement in doing this was Iceland's Kitchenware Revolution that resulted not only in strong measures against "banksters" who had caused a deep economic crisis, but also the drafting of a new constitution using extensive crowdsourcing. Some 16,000 suggestions and comments received and debated using social networks. But despite being approved by a two-thirds majority in a referendum, this "Wiki-Constitution" was stalled in parliament by various maneuvers of the opposition.[22]

The content of the diverse messages of the Brazilian protesters, both online and in massive demonstrations, and how to deal with them began to be analyzed and debated in the Brazilian press and online in June 2013.[23] A number of observers have pointed out that political parties are indispensable to mediate and aggregate these demands – but the protesters overwhelmingly reject their representatives. The above-mentioned IBOPE poll of demonstrators found that 83% of them felt that no politician represented them, 89% declared that no political party represented them, 86% said they did not belong to a union, professional association or student entity, and 96% were not affiliated with any party.[24]

Manuel Castells, Director of the Interdisciplinary Internet Institute of the Open University of Catalonia (Spain) and Professor at the Annenberg School of Communication at the University of Southern California (USC), has analyzed a number of network-mobilized protest movements that occurred prior to those that emerged in Turkey and Brazil in 2013 in his book *Networks of Outrage and Hope: Social Movements in the Internet Age.*[25] Castells describes some common elements of these movements that also characterize the Brazilian protests.

> "The movements spread by contagion in a world networked by the wireless Internet and marked by fast, viral diffusion of images and ideas. They started in the South and in the North, in Tunisia and Iceland, and from there the spark lit the fire in a diverse social landscape devastated by greed and manipulation in all quarters of the blue planet. It was not just poverty, or the economic crisis, or the lack of democracy that caused the multifaceted rebellion. Of course, all these poignant manifestations of an unjust society and of an undemocratic polity were present in the protests. But it was primarily the humiliation provoked by the cynicism and arrogance of those

in power, be it financial, political or cultural, that brought together those who turned fear into outrage, and outrage into hope for a better humanity."[26]

In Brazil some government agencies, seeking to become more responsive to citizen needs, have encouraged online participation in policymaking – examples in Brazil are the online participatory budgeting in cities such as Porto Alegre and Anatel's submission of proposed regulations online for comment prior to public meetings before promulgation of revised versions of the regulations. A prime example is the drafting process for the Civil Rights Framework for the Internet (*Marco Civil da Internet*) that will be discussed in detail in Chapter 7.

The Law of Access to Information (Law 12,257 of 11 November 2011), that became effective in May 2012, established open access to government information at all three levels of Brazil's federal structure as the default option, with exceptions needing to be justified and appealable, effectively reversing the previous order. Special access to information pages have been established by many government units, but it remains to be seen how effective this law will be.

Around the world techniques of eGovernment, eLegislature, eJudiciary, eEducation, eHealth, eBusiness, etc. are becoming increasingly sophisticated and interactive: they have moved from simple "publishing" of information to making available searchable data bases, promoting citizen- and consumer-centric participatory interactions, allowing complete online economic or document transactions, and even facilitating an "all of government" approach to meeting citizen needs. In government, this involves breaking down internal ministerial or agency silos to deliver government services needed and wanted by citizens in simplified and convenient fashion. This saves users time and money as well as bettering citizen perceptions of government and business.[27]

Digital Inclusion, Telecenters, and Lanhouses

In 1995, Rodrigo Baggio launched the Committee for Democracy in Information Technology (*Comitê de Democratização da Informática* – CDI) in Rio de Janeiro. With initial support from IBASE and then various community, philanthropic, private sector organizations, CDI developed Schools for Computer Science and Citizenship (*Escolas de Informática e Cidadania* – EIC) that became increasingly Internet oriented. Charging a small, symbolic fee to their students, they spread rapidly and by 2004 numbered 830 in 20 Brazilian states and 10 other countries.[28]

Then in 2000 a new movement arose in São Paulo, with support of the state and municipal governments. Telecenters, or infocenters (there are other names), may be loosely defined as free public Internet access points usually offering digital literacy training sometimes including web site construction and support for the generally low-income communities in which they are located. They first began in Europe and the United States in the mid 1980s and spread to many countries. In Brazil they numbered over 8000 by the end of 2010. Annual national workshops of the telecenter movement were held in different Brazilian cities. In these workshops the movement developed its approach to digital inclusion, shared experience, and sought some coordination. At the federal level various ministries and the *Banco do Brasil* had their own telecenter programs, but these programs were not well coordinated.[29]

Paid public Internet access points, called cyber cafés or lanhouses, or more recently "centers of digital inclusion" were far more numerous and had had a much greater proportion of total internet users than free telecenters for every year since CETIC. br began its annual surveys, even among poorest socio-economic classes, D and E. These lanhouses and cyber cafés were mostly small, family-owned, often informal businesses. They provide Internet access, usually with little instruction, where users are free to browse as they wish and use any online applications (e.g. e-mail, social networks, Skype, and online games), unlike in many telecenters, where access to some sites and applications may be blocked. Lanhouses often sell other goods and services such as computer equipment, fax, printing, and scanning.[30] The estimated number of lanhouses was 108,000 at the end of 2009, but by the end of 2012 some 48,000 had gone out of business as the percentage of internauts with home access increased and the weaker ones failed.[31]

Looking at the CETIC.br national data, the most striking trend is the steady increase in users who access the Internet from their homes over the eight years for which the surveys were available in February 2014. As for public access points, there was consistently a far greater percentage of users accessing the internet from lanhouses and cyber cafés than free public access points, and this was true both for the total number of users and for those in the poorest socio-economic classes (D and E). Also notable is the rise and then fall in the percentage of users for both paid and unpaid public access public access centers (Table 3).

Table 3: Percentage of Total Internet Users by
Place of Access, 2005, 2010, and 2012

Place of Access	2005	2010	2012
In home, total	42	56	74
In home, classes DE	8	14	35
Paid Public Access Center total	18	35	19
Paid public access center, classes DE	30	67	42
Free public access center total	2	4	4
Free public access center, classes DE	3	6	4

Sources: CETIC.br surveys, Table C6
(2005); Table C4 (2010 & 2012)

Lack of a national eTransformation strategy

The lack of a national eTransformation strategy has resulted in insufficient and poorly coordinated government policies and under-investment in critical infrastructure. The only official attempt to justify and develop such a strategy was a report published in 2000 and entitled *Information Society in Brazil: Green Book*. It was produced by a team at the Ministry of Science and Technology led by Tadao Takahashi.[32]

This impressive document was elaborated with contributions from hundreds of specialists, and was described by the then Minister of Science and Technology, Ronaldo Sardemberg, as "a nationwide strategic project to integrate and coordinate the development and employment of advanced computer, communication and information technologies and their applications in society. This endeavor will allow the government to further research and education, as well as assure that the Brazilian economy is capable of competing on the world market." The "green book", as it was called, proposed "a series of actions to advance and foster the Information Society in Brazil in all of its aspects: expansion of access, means of connectivity, training of human resources, incentives for research and development, electronic commerce, development of new applications."[33] The program was never implemented.

The e-Brasil project – an undertaking of some 70 Brazilian and international specialists from government, academia, civil society and private sector companies – sought to encourage the development of such a strategy at the federal, state, and municipal levels in two publications in 2006 to 2007.[34] Takahashi, who had continued his effort to develop a national ICT strategy as a consultant after leaving the MCT, made a major contribution to the e-Brasil project.[35] As noted in the foreword to this book, it is difficult to gauge the project's success.

The digital cities movement

In the absence of any overall national strategy for using ICT to accelerate development, some small municipalities started to develop their own strategies. They became known as Digital Cities, though the definition of this term is quite flexible, ranging from the provision of free Internet service to a comprehensive effort to use ICTs as an accelerator of socio-economic development.

The digital cities movement began in Europe and the United States in the 1990s. The first Brazilian digital city was a small town of less than 8,000 inhabitants located over 600 km from the capital of São Paulo state, Sud Mennucci. In 2002 the mayor of that city, that had no ISP, decided to build a tower and mount Wi-Fi antennas on it, connected to the Internet by a commercial link provided by Telefônica. The next year the mayor decided to open the Wi-Fi network to any citizen.

A more structured approach to building a digital city, with a clear comprehensive strategy behind it, was developed in Piraí, a municipality some 130 km from the Rio de Janeiro along the highway linking Rio de Janeiro and São Paulo. In February 2004, under the leadership of the then mayor, Luiz Fernandes de Souza, better known as Pezão, a system of wired and wireless Internet connectivity linking the municipal government buildings, telecenters, schools, health posts, libraries and some public spaces (e.g. the bus station) was inaugurated.

A systematic program to use ICT to further the socio-economic development of Piraí, especially in the schools, was conceived and implemented by teams led by two university professors born in Piraí, Franklin Dias Coelho and Maria Helena Jardim.[36] In 2009 Piraí became the first municipality to have one computer per student and the city has won a number of national and international awards. In 2010, Mayor Pezão was elected Vice Governor of the State of Rio de Janeiro. [37]

Piraí's example was followed by other municipalities in the state of Rio de Janeiro and elsewhere in Brazil, though the approach in many of these was less comprehensive, often limited to providing free public Wi-Fi access. A program was initiated in the MC to expand the number of digital cities, but for some years was limited to a number of pilot projects. It did not really take off until after the launch of the PNBL. In 2012 80 cities were selected for the Digital Cities Program. By that time the MC had defined digital cities as those having a fiber optic network and:

- Internet links between all public entities;
- implementation of software for managing finances, tax collection, health and education;
- training of civil servants in the use of ICT and specialized software; and
- public Internet access points in squares, bus stations, and other spaces.[38]

Chapter 3: Development of the Internet in Brazil

1   See Jensen (2011) for another, partially overlapping, analysis of broadband development in Brazil through 2010.

2   Brazilian Internet Steering Committee (2013) is the latest in this increasingly detailed set of statistics and accompanying analyses based on sample surveys similar to those of the Brazilian Institute of Geography and Statistics' (IBGE) National Household Sample Survey (PNAD). All CETIC.br survey data is available online at http://www.cetic.br/. IBGE's PNAD data is also available at http://www.ibge. gov.br/home/estatistica/pesquisas/pesquisa_resultados. php?id_pesquisa=40. Both sites accessed 24 January 2014.

3   CETIC.br defines broadband as any connection above the maximum available via a dialup connection, that is above 64 kbps. Apparently this definition is used more broadly in Brazil. CETIC.br statistics are available for various speeds, but large numbers of households surveyed (26% of those with Internet access in 2012) either don't know or or did not reply to the question regarding speed of their connection.

4   Telebrasil press release http://www.telebrasil.org.br/sala-de-imprensa/releases/5315-brasil-fecha-2013-com-133-milhoes-de-acessos-em-banda-larga. 31 January, 2004. Accessed 1 February 2014.

5   http://teleco.com.br/3g_cobertura.asp. Accessed 30 January 2014.

6   http://www.teleco.com.br/3g_brasil.asp. Accessed 30 January 2014.

7   http://www.teleco.com.br/4g_cobertura.asp. Accessed 30 January 2014.

8   http://www.teleco.com.br/ncel.asp. Accessed 30 January 2014.

9   http://www.oecd.org/sti/broadband/oecdbroadbandportal.htm. Accessed 30 January 2014.

10   All the reports downloadable in both Portuguese and English versions at http://www.cetic.br/publicacoes/index.htm.

11   Facebook statistics from http://www.quintly.com/blog/2013/03/facebook-country-statistics-march-2013/. Accessed 31 January 2014.

12   http://www.rediff.com/business/slide-show/slide-show-1-special-15-countries-that-have-most-twitter-users/20131009.htm#16. Accessed 2 February 2014.

13   http://www.slideshare.net/linkhumans/linkedin-usage-by-country-july-2013-by-link-humans. Accessed 2 February 2014.

14   Comscore (2013).

15   The quotes in this section are from interviews conducted with participants in the 2013 annual meeting of Abrint.

16   Smith (2011), p. 6.

17   Castells (2012).

18   http://g1.globo.com/brasil/noticia/2013/06/veja-integra-da-pesquisa-do-ibope-sobre-os-manifestantes.html. Accessed 2 February 2014.

19   ITU (2013), Table 2.2, p. 143.

20   For a detailed account of how social media were used to help organize the overthrow of Egypt's President Mubarak by one of the movement's leaders, see Ghonim (2012). A broader study of network-based social movements in a large number of countries can be found in Castells (2012).

21   IBOPE Inteligência (2013)

22   Castells (2012), especially pp. 30-44 and Thorvaldur (2013).

23   See, for example, Bernard Sorj, "A política além da internet", http://www.schwartzman.org.br/sitesimon/?p=4520&lang=pt-br. Accessed 28 January 2014.

24   http://g1.globo.com/brasil/noticia/2013/06/veja-integra-da-pesquisa-do-ibope-sobre-os-manifestantes.html. Accessed 2 February 2014.

25   Castells (2012).

26 Ibid, p. 2.

27 For an analisis of such developments in Brazil and seven other countries, see Hanna & Knight (2011 and 2012).

28 See Baggio and De Luca (2004) and http://www.cdi.org.br, accessed 1 March 2014.

29 See Falavigna & Mori (2004) and Falavigna (2011) for the history and philosophy/ideology of telecenters in Brazil.

30 Almeida (2013).

31 Ibid.

32 Takahashi (2000).

33 Ibid, p. v.

34 Knight & Fernandes (2006), and Knight, Fernandes, & Cunha (2007).

35 Takahashi (2007).

36 See Coelho (2007) for an analytical approach to digital cities in Brazil.

37 See http://www.piraidigital.com.br/ for information on current projects

38 http://www.mc.gov.br/inclusao-digital/acoes-e-programas/cidades-digitais. Accessed 9 February 2014.

Chapter 4

Speed, Cost, and Quality

Brazil ranks poorly on various indicators of Internet service for rich countries and some not so rich. But looking at the BRICS (Brazil, Russia, India, China, and South Africa) and two of the larger Latin American countries (Argentina and Mexico), Brazil is not doing so badly as measured by well-respected international indexes: the International Telecommunications Union (ITU) ICT Development Index (IDI), the IDI's Access sub-index, and the World Economic Forum/INSEAD Network Readiness Index (NRI). All of these indicators measure more than Internet access, and the interested reader can consult the definitions of each.[1] But none of these countries come close to Korea's ranking (Table 4)

Table 4: Comparison of Brazil's Rank with Those of Selected Countries on IDI, IDI Access Component and NRI, 2012

Country	IDI	IDA – Access	NRI
Brazil	62	67	60
Russia	40	37	54
India	121	122	68
China	78	80	58
South Africa	84	85	70
Argentina	53	56	99

Country	IDI	IDA – Access	NRI
Mexico	83	87	63
Korea, Rep.	1	11	11

Sources: ITU (2013) for IDI (Table 2.2, p. 24)
and IDA Access (Table 2.6, p. 46), Bilbat-Osorio,
Dutta, & Lavin (2013) for NRI (p. xxi).

Nevertheless, Brazil's networks are slow, expensive, and often unreliable. In this chapter these assertions are documented, and some of the reasons for this state of affairs explored.

Connection speed

Using Akami's statistics on the speed of connections to its webservers, the average connection speed for Brazil in the third quarter of 2013 was 2.7 million bits per second (Mbps), 75% of the global average, lower than Russia and China, above India and South Africa, slightly below Argentina and Mexico, but way below Korea's 22.1 Mbps. In Brazil 20% of the connections were above 4 Mbps, compared with 33% for Mexico, and 93% for South Korea. For mobile connections, Brazil's average speed was 1.1 Mbps. The percentage of users with connection speeds above 10 Mbps was 0.9% for Brazil, better than India (0.3) but less than the other BRICS and Mexico, and badly lagging Korea's 93% (Table 5). The faster the velocity, the better and more efficient is use of the Internet.

Table 5: Comparison of Brazil's Connection Speeds
with those of Selected Countries, 3rd Quarter 2013

Country	Av. Speed (Mbps)	% Above 4 Mbps	% Above 10 Mbps
Brazil	2.7	20	0.9
Russia	7.8	73	24
India	1.4	3	0.3
China	2.9	20	1.1
South Africa	2.3	7.7	1.1
Argentina	2.8	18	0.9
Mexico	3.9	33	1.7
Korea, Rep.	22.1	93	70

Source: Akami (2014)

Fixed and mobile broadband prices

Prices, while falling, are still very high. In a recent study comparing the monthly average cost per Mbps capacity in 15 countries in 2012, Brazil was the second highest with an average cost of US$25, exceeded only by Argentina (US$46). Compare this, for example, with Chile (US$23), Portugal (US$11), United States (US$3.33), Finland (US$2.77), and South Korea (US$0.27).[2]

A 2013 study by the ITU compared prices for fixed and mobile Internet service in 2012 for all countries from which price data could be obtained. Prices were measured both in US$ and as a percentage of monthly gross national income per capita, a rough index of affordability. For fixed-line broadband Brazil ranked number 55, at US$17.80 for an entry-level broadband subscription that cost the user 2% of per capita GNI. For prepaid mobile handset data package with 500 MB/month included, the price was US$38.5 or 4% of monthly GNI per capita, with Brazil ranking 75th out of 126 countries (some 80% of Brazilian cellphones are prepaid).[3]

International price comparisons have to be used with caution, since the speeds are those advertised (in Brazil at the time of the studies mentioned, actual instantaneous bandwidth delivered was allowed to be as low as 20% of the advertised bandwidth (for both downloads and uploads) or an average of 60% of the advertised speed over a month of measurements. Also, for fixed-line service, the price used in the ITU survey was for an entry-level (lowest priced) connection, the speed of which varies considerably between countries. In the case of Brazil an entry-level connection under the National Broadband Program (*Programa Nacional de Banda Larga - PNBL*), explained in detail in Chapter 5, is 1 Mbps. For mobile connections, the actual prices paid in Brazil may be lower as many customers use phones with two or more SIM cards to take advantage of cheaper rates for calling within an operator's own network. This being said, the average prices paid by Brazilians are still high.

The high cost of telecommunications services in Brazil is influenced by three factors: excessive taxation, high interconnection fees and domestic content regulations. Excessive charges for leasing transmission capacity where a provider lacks its own infrastructure also contribute.

Excessive Taxation

The telecommunications sector bears the highest tax burden of any sector. In ten states and the Federal District the ICMS tax (Tax on Circulation of Goods and Delivery of Services) alone is 25% of the gross price, for others it is as high as the 35% imposed in Rondônia. Most taxes are calculated on the gross revenue, e.g. telephone bills, including all these taxes. For the states with a 25% ICMS, the main tributes (Cofins, PIS/PASEP, ICMS, Fust, and Funtel) equal 30% of the total bill, but if calculated as rates on telecommunications bills net of these taxes, the rate is 43%. And in states with higher ICMS rates the total tax burden on net revenue is even higher, reaching a maximum of 49% in Rondônia.[4]

In addition to these taxes, there are fees for a new cellphone number (TFI, R$26.83) and an annual maintenance fee (TFF, R$13.42). Since about 80% of cellphones use the prepaid system, and these are mostly used by poorer people, these taxes are extremely regressive. Add this to the much higher unit cost of "low cost" data packages, and the regressiveness is even greater. Consider further that not only is the unit cost of data packages lower for larger data packages, but the cost of any smartphone purchased at a reduced price as part of a contract falls the larger the size of the data package purchased, yet another regressive feature.

Additional taxes and charges are imposed on the telecommunications operators as well, but these are not unique to the telecommunications sector. Taxes on telecommunications services in 2012 totaled some R$59.2 billion of which R$7.4 billion were for Fust, Fistel, and Funttel, and R$51.8 billion from the above-mentioned taxes plus other taxes collected indirectly on capital expenditures totaling R$25.3 billion, leaving net profits of R$10.9 billion. Taxes and the funds took up 30.8% of operational revenue, and dividends to shareholders 4.8%.[5] The tax issue is discussed further in Chapter 5.

High interconnection fees

The fees charged when calls are transferred between different carriers, and between fixed line and mobile phones, are very high. Excessive inter-carrier fees lead to the use of mobile phones that can use multiple SIM cards. Another effect of the high interconnection fees is that they encourage the use of pre-paid plans for mobile phones. Indeed, 78% of mobile lines were prepaid as of January 2014. For these the costs per minute are exorbitant, though they can be mitigated by making calls within a given carrier's own network. In-network calls are much cheaper since the carriers don't have to pay interconnection charges. This has led many users to own multiple cellphones, or use phones that can carry multiple SIM cards.

Prepaid phones are usually used by poor people only to receive calls, since in Brazil the caller pays. As the interconnection fees are higher than the price per minute of calls from prepaid plans, a prepaid plan user who never makes a call, but receives interconnected calls, becomes more lucrative for the operators than one using a postpaid plan. Inter-carrier transfer fees are being reduced by Anatel by two-thirds between 2012 and 2015 as part of the General Plan for Competition Goals (*Plano Geral de Metas de Competição* – PGMC).[6] Until then, interconnection fees in Brazil will still be among the highest in the world.

Requirements for domestic content in production and technology use

The price of computers, telecommunications equipment, smartphones, and new fiber lines are all inflated by domestic content requirements – including those recently imposed to qualify for exemptions from some federal taxes, as discussed in Chapter 5. In addition, when government agencies, including state enterprises like Telebras, make purchases, bidders selling domestically assembled products are allowed to have prices

15% higher than imported goods, and if domestic technology is used, the preference rises to 25%.[7] Such requirements, intended to promote the development of Brazil's equipment industry, also tend to boost the cost and usually lower the quality of equipment to users, though reliable statistical estimates of these costs are not available. Measures adopted in 2013 attempt to reduce costs by cutting taxes for new broadband network projects (see Chapter 5).

Service quality

Besides being expensive and slow, customer service in Brazilian telecommunications inspires many complaints. Mobile telephony and data services are prone to dropped calls. It got so bad that Anatel suspended the sale of SIM cards by TIM in 19 states, Oi in five, and Claro in three in July 2012, requiring them to present detailed state-by-state improvements plans, with special attention to dropped connections and customer service. In September of 2012 Anatel accepted the operators plans and the sale of new lines was again permitted. The other providers, Vivo, SBTC and Sercomtel, were also required to present improvement plans. Anatel monitors fulfillment of these plans on a quarterly basis using a series of metrics, including multiple network performance indicators, customer service, dropped mobile connections, and investments under a three-year investment plan.

Sales of mobile devices

Despite the cost and quality issues, wireless broadband coverage has been growing fast as shown in Chapter 3. And sales of both smartphones and tablets have exploded. In the first three quarters of 2013 alone, 24.1 million smartphone were sold in Brazil, up 117% over the same period in 2012. To this add 7.9 million tablets sold in 2013, an increase of 142% over 2012.[8] Smartphones and tablets are in fact handheld computers that can access the web and also do free video and audio conferencing and text chat over wireless connections to the Internet. With the rapid fall in prices for smartphones and tablets using Google's Android system, they have in fact become accessible to lower-middle class (Class C in Brazilian marketing parlance) and even to poor people (Classes D and E) for the lower-priced models.

Chapter 4: Speed, Cost, and Quality

1 ITU (2013) and Bilbat-Osorio, Dutta, & Lavin (2013).

2 http://economia.uol.com.br/noticias/redacao/2013/05/14/banda-larga-no-brasil-e-a-2-mais-cara-entre-15-paises-diz-pesquisa.htm. Accessed 2 February 2014. This article is based on research by Samy Dana and Victor Candido.

3 ITU (2013), Tables 3.2 and 3.1, pp 82 and100, respectively. Accessed 2 February 2014.

4 http://www.teleco.com.br/tributos.asp. Accessed 2 February 2014.

5 Telebrasil (2013), p. 64.

6 See Mattos (2014) for an extensive and up-to-date analysis of interconnection charges and recent Anatel policies adopted to deal with the problem.

7 http://www.telesintese.com.br/index.php/plantao/25382-regulamentada-o-uso-da-margem-de-preferencia-nas-compras-publicas-de-tics. Accessed 14 February 2014.

8 http://www.emarketer.com/Article/Cheaper-Devices-Boost-Tablet-Sales-Brazil/1010487. Accessed 2 February 2014

Chapter 5

What Is Being Done to Improve Internet Connectivity?

The lack of a holistic national strategy to promote eTransformation that spans all sectors of government and the economy as well as still insufficient priority in public policy and investments are serious problems. They have held back the development of applications that require fast and reliable connectivity and higher rates of Internet penetration to deliver better public services, help reduce income inequality, accelerate economic growth, and improve Brazil's competitiveness in the global economy. But looking more narrowly at Internet service provision, in recent years considerable progress has been achieved in improving network infrastructure and both fixed and mobile Internet service. This chapter looks at what has been accomplished to achieve these objectives.

The National Broadband Program

The first serious attempt to implement a national broadband policy and program, other than the academic Internet run by the RNP, now the National Education and Research Network (*Rede Nacional de Ensino e Pesquisa*), was the PNBL enacted by Presidential Decree 7.175 of 12 May 2010. PNBL objectives, according to its basic document, are to:

- accelerate the entry of the population into the modern information society;
- promote greater access to e-government services to citizens and to facilitate the use of state services;
- contribute to the evolution of telecommunications networks in the country, through the adoption of current trends in technology and architecture, based on communications over IP;
- contribute to the industrial and technological development of the country – particularly the sector of Information and Communication Technologies;
- improve the competitiveness of Brazilian companies, especially those in the ICT sector, as well as micro, small and medium enterprises of other economic sectors;
- contribute to the increase of employment opportunities in the country; and
- contribute to the growth of the Brazilian economy.[1]

One of the principal instruments for executing the PNBL is Telebras, the federal telecommunications company that had been dormant since the privatization of the state telephone companies in 1998 and is supervised by the Ministry of Communications. In 2010 Telebras was resurrected for this purpose. Large private telecommunications companies opposed this. Their representatives argued that a better policy would be to use tax reductions to expand market demand. Auctions where the winner would be the company asking for the lowest subsidy to achieve coverage objectives that normal market competition would not attain, a model used in Chile and other countries, could also be used. Such subsidies could be financed, at least in part, by Fust.

The federal government preferred to use Telebras to help bring down prices, as well as selective tax reductions, the latter always encountering resistance from the Finance Ministry. Another way of meeting coverage targets adopted was to require bidders in wireless spectrum auctions to meet coverage targets, though that policy reduced revenues from the auctions, since providers factored in the cost of meeting these targets in making their bids.

Since the PNBL was launched, the federal, state and municipal governments as well as Telebras have given greater priority to network expansion. The National Agency for Electric Energy (Agência Nacional de Energia Elelétrica – Aneel), the electricity regulator, plays a key role by ruling over power generating and distributing companies. The large companies in the Eletrobras system have extensive fiber optic networks using what are called Optical Ground Wires (OPGW) hung from pylons that carry high-voltage lines and frequently used for internal control purposes. But since very little capacity is needed for this purpose, these cables also contain unlit (dark) fiber that can be leased to telecommunications operators, including RNP.

State-level public power distribution companies have similar high-voltage lines, and also lower-voltage lines strung on poles that can also carry fiber optic cables be used to develop a "smart grid" to improve efficiency in the use of electric power, but with enough fibers to allow leasing them to one or more telecommunications companies. Or a telco could hang the cables and lease capacity to the power company and/or other telcos.

Small and medium telecommunications operators are pushing Anatel to approve a resolution passed by Aneel in August 2013 that would set rules for the rental of space on these poles, rules that would result in lower rents. In the meantime, Telebras contracted for the use of poles at prices well above those proposed by the Aneel resolution.[2] This is another example of uncoordinated sectoral policies.

Despite receiving considerably less investment resources than announced on various occasions by government officials (that can be considered a sign of less than urgent priority for the PNBL), Telebras has gradually created a national network of fiber optic cables, in large part through public-public and public-private partnerships that involve leasing or exchanging existing dark fiber. In 2011 Telebras established long-term rental contracts for use of fiber some 16,000 km in the OPGW cables of electric power companies that are run by Eletronet, a company that is owned by Eletrobras and AES, an American company.[3] Telebras also leased some 2,200 km of fiber from Petrobras. Another 2,200 km were obtained in an exchange of use of fiber with a private operator, TIM, in 2013. These arrangements allowed expansion of Telebras trunk lines in rings that provide redundant links in case of failure at any point in the system. Likewise Telebras has arranged swaps of dark fiber on RNP's Redecomep networks (see Chapter 5) for dark fiber on its own backbone network.[4]

Telebras is also investing in its own fiber optic links to provide high capacity redundant links to the six cities where the Confederations Cup soccer matches were played in 2013 and to the 12 cities that will host the World Cup matches in 2014. Figure 5 shows the Telebras network in 2014 as projected in 2012.

Figure 5: The Telebras Backbone Network
in 2014 as Projected in 2012

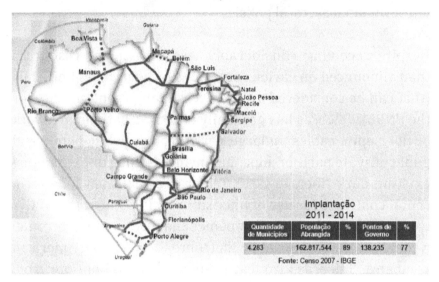

Source: Presentation by Caio Bonilha to
Futurecom Conference, 10 October 2012

Traditional private telecommunications providers complement Telebras in implementation of the PNBL. ISPs that offer access of at least 1 Mbps to their customers at PNB prices – R$35 (US$15) or R$29 (US$12) in states that have eliminated the ICMS on PNBL subscriptions – qualify for wholesale bandwidth from Telebrás at below-market prices.

Small and medium ISPs and the large operators – like Oi, Telefônica, Embratel, TIM, and Algar Telecom – offer the PNBL packages, in some cases benefiting from state tax exemptions. The operators are discovering that many PNBL customers soon want faster and more expensive connections. In this way, the PNBL is opening new markets for the private operators.

The growth of the Telebras network has increased competition and thereby led to lower prices offered by private providers.

Telebras says it has not cut the wholesale prices it charges as far as it could and still cover costs so as not to drive the private operators, needed for meeting Internet penetration goals, out of the market.[5] The federal government encourages private operators to expand digital inclusion of populations in underserved markets. Under the voluntary adoption of PNBL pricing, by the end of 2012 the number of basic 1 Mbps connections under the PNBL had reached 2.5 million (13% of all fixed broadband connections) in 2850 municipalities.[6]

Telebras is also investing in a Brazilian geostationary satellite that would provide military X band and civilian Ka band communications covering all of Brazil's territory. The satellite is expected to be launched toward the end of 2015. Telebras also has plans for submarine fiber optic cables to Africa, Europe, and the United States to reduce costs for Internet connectivity. It is unclear whether the necessary resources will be forthcoming to undertake these investments.

Small entrepreneurs like Adilson Klaffke of Nova Guarita in Mato Grosso were often the first to provide Internet service to remote communities. The number of these firms has doubled in the last two years as a result of the PNBL and simplified and cheaper procedures for acquiring Multimedia Communications Services (*Serviço de Comunicação Multimídia* - SCM) licenses from Anatel.

Expansion of high-speed connections has been spurred by growth in demand for Internet access by the emerging lower middle class. This group tends to provide voting support for the government, but also is courted by opposition parties. These new consumers are buying smartphones, tablets, and laptops (encouraged by exemptions from taxes on production of these products as discussed below) and want broadband connections.

Expansion of the RNP: The Redecomep and Veredas Novas Programs

Since its early days, the RNP has expanded in scope and speed. The current backbone network, called *Rede Ipê*, is extensive and continues to grow. As of February 2014 it had points of presence (POPs) in all 26 states and the Federal District. Of these POPs, those in 23 states and the Federal District have connections faster than 1 Gbps. RNP also has links with academic networks in 14 other Latin American countries, Internet 2 in the United States, and Géant in Europe, as well as with the global Internet (Figure 6).

Figure 6: RNP's Backbone Network in December 2013

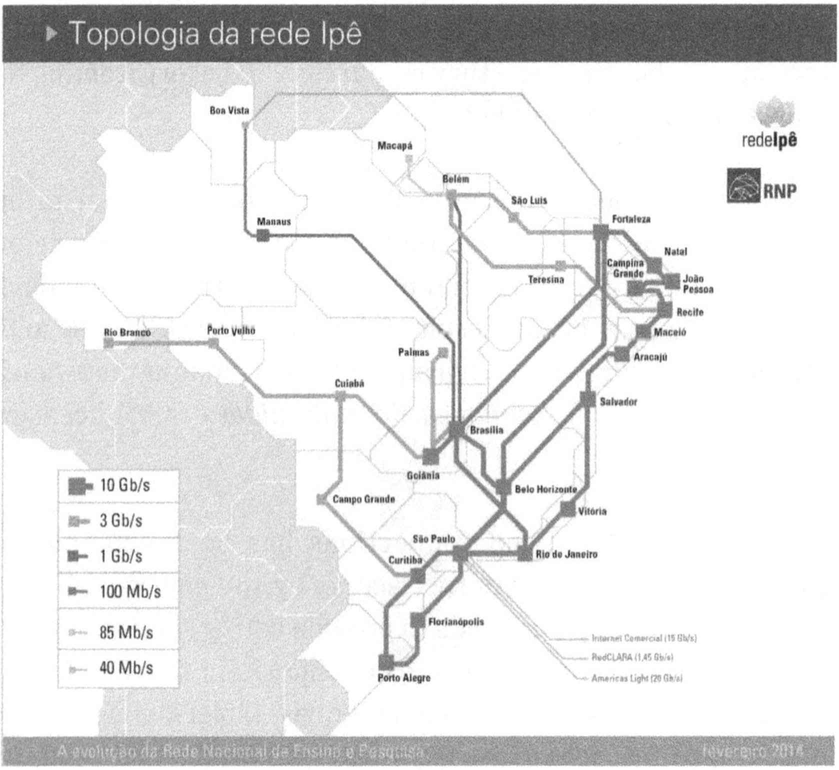

Source: RNP

In 2005 RNP began a new program to build fast metropolitan fiber optic networks in Brazil's major cities in association with a variety of partners. This program is called Redecomep, and as of February 2014 had 24 community networks in operation and another 17 under construction.

The Ministry of Science, Technology and Innovation (MCTI) finances fiber optic cables and equipment for operation of the fibers in these cables that serve academic and research institutions. But the number of pairs of fiber in these cables is much larger than needed for the academic and research institutions, allowing allocation to other partners that provide services in kind or direct leasing payments. For example, metros, light rail lines, urban toll roads, and state and municipal governments can offer rights of way and ducts. Electric power companies can provide poles on which the cables can be hung. And Telebras can offer fibers in its backbone network.

These partners are responsible for investing their own resources for lighting their fibers, routing traffic, building extensions to serve their own clients, and sharing operations and maintenance costs. The advantage these partners gain is usually cheaper bandwidth than available from commercial operators. For RNP, in addition to providing connectivity for educational and research institutions, the partnerships can cover most if not all costs for operation and maintenance of the metropolitan networks, making them financially sustainable.

RNP's newest program is called *Veredas Novas* (New Paths). It is a joint program with MCTI, MC, the Ministry of Education, and Telebras. Its objective is to provide fiber connections to research and educational institutions in the interior of the states, and also digital inclusion of the as yet unserved population in the vicinity of these institutions. In each city RNP is establishing a local access point, with radio and eventually fiber connections to ISPs that agree to offer Internet service of at least 1 Mbps at PNBL prices. These ISPs can also offer faster connections at market prices.

The program's goals, as set forth in 2012, were to reach 250 locations with 335 institutions by the end of 2014.[7] Minimum speeds to major institutions are to be 1 Gbps, to smaller ones, 100 Mbps. This should make it possible to store data and collections of scientific and technological works in the cloud. High-speed links to research networks outside Brazil are included, facilitated by a new submarine cable to Africa and Europe. The program appears unlikely to meet these goals so soon. Partnerships with state networks described below appear to be one way to accelerate the program, and some such partnerships are being undertaken, beginning with Ceará.

Figure 7: The *Veredas Novas* Program
Expands the *RNP Backbone* Network

Source:RNP

State fiber optic and wireless networks

To obtain cheaper broadband service, several states are building their own fiber optic networks outside the capitals. The leaders are Pará and Ceará.

Pará's Navegapará program goes beyond Belém's MetroBel network initiated by RNP and expanded by the state's ICT company, Prodepa. In 2013 Navegapará reached 62 of Pará's 144 municipalities with some 1200 km of fiber cables (Figure 8) using partnerships with the state electric power company (Celpa) and Eletronorte (a company in the Eletrobras group). Navegapará's fiber network is being expanded further.

Figure 8: Navegapará's Fiber Optic Network in 2012

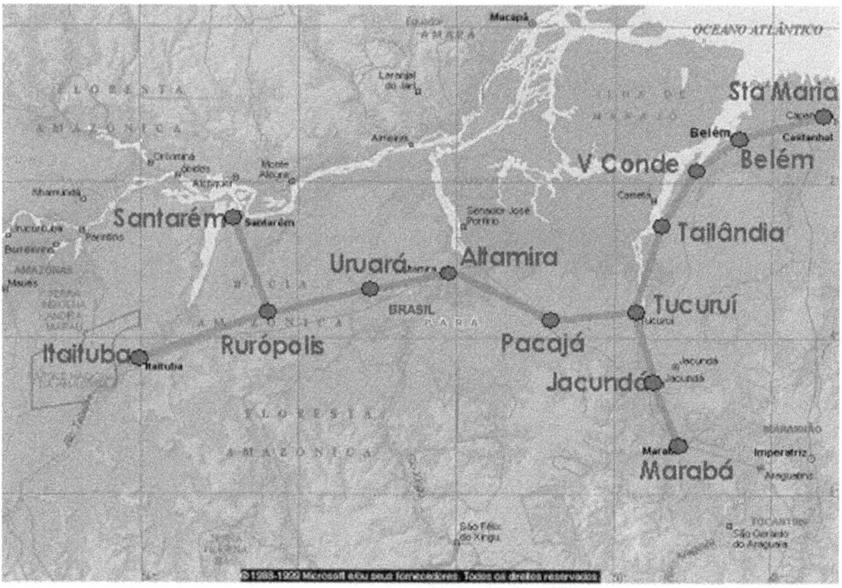

Source: Adapted from presentation by Leila Daher, Prodepa

In Ceará the state ICT company, Etice, has built a 3,000-kilometer ring of fiber optic cables around the state that, with its wireless extensions, reaches 88 percent of the state's population. Called the Digital Belt (*Cinturão Digital*), its nucleus is Gigafor, co-financed by RNP's Redecomep program in Fortaleza. At various points along the fiber trunk lines there are towers from which municipalities not on the Digital Belt can connect through wireless links, allowing them to communicate with the state government and other municipalities (Figure 9). As of February 2014 Etice had two partners in the Digital Belt – RNP and the state power company, Coelce. There are plans to expand the Digital Belt to reach more interior points in the state as part of contracts to be signed with future private sector partners and the RNP's *Veredas Novas* program.

Figure 9: Ceará's Digital Belt

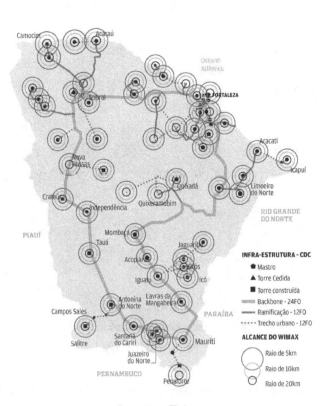

Source: Etice

A fundamental characteristic of these growing state networks is partnerships between the RNP, electric power companies, municipal governments, private telecommunications operators, and, more recently, Telebras.

Among the characteristics of the best state and municipal networks are:

- the state or municipality takes advantage of dark fiber allocated to it in the state capital's Redecomep;
- partnerships are established with RNP, municipalities, state and federal public enterprises, private telecoms, and Telebras to extend the network's reach and share costs of operation and maintenance;
- complementary fiber and wireless networks are built to fill in gaps and provide capillarity (urban as well as rural);
- maintenance and operation are outsourced to private firms; and
- states or municipalities have the option to lease dark fiber in their networks to private operators to generate additional revenue, helping to cover operating and maintenance costs.

In Paraná the state government has used another route to building a state network, namely purchasing bandwidth from Copel Telecom, a subsidiary of the state electric power company. Copel Telecom has an extensive fiber optic network launched in 2010 that by the end of 2012 reached all 399 municipalities in the state.

Tax Reform

Punishing taxes and fees, while easy to collect, are regressive, and run contrary to the government's goal of digital inclusion.

They may have made some sense when telephone service was limited to high-income individuals and businesses and monopoly telcos made it easy to collect the taxes. But today telephone service either mobile or fixed is almost universal, at least in urban areas, and taxes are much easier to collect with electronic invoices mandatory in much of the country.

The enormous tax burden imposed on telecommunications services goes against any economic logic. First, taxing a highly strategic sector for Brazil's competitiveness in the global knowledge-based economy puts Brazil at a disadvantage. Second, this over-taxation runs totally contrary to the digital inclusion objectives of the federal, state, and municipal governments, even more so since the taxation is highly regressive. Third, a good case can be made that the price elasticity of demand for telecommunication services and the equipment necessary to use them, at least for lower and middle-income individuals and most enterprises, is positive, high and in many cases may be more than one. This means that is a fall in prices to consumers of one percent would result in more than a one percent increase in demand, opening the possibility that reducing tax rates could actually increase tax revenue, or at least the percentage fall would be considerably less than percentage reduction in taxes.

In sum, this heavy taxation of telecommunications lessens ICT's potential to reduce inequality and accelerate economic development. Current over-taxation of telecommunications is an urgent priority. But so far attempts to reduce it have in large part failed.

The MC has reviewed three separate studies done over the period 2008-2010 that support the hypothesis of a high price elasticity of demand, and in 2012 made its own estimates that are based on data from CETIC.br's 2011 household survey. The estimates ranged from 1.0 to 3.36, with MC's own study came up with a value of 1.45. MC then proposed that the four federal tributes on broadband services (PIS, Cofins, Fust and Funttel) be reduced to zero and that state ICMS rates be lowered from an average of 26.7% to a uniform 10%, resulting in a 24% fall in prices, assuming all the reductions were passed on to consumers.

Assuming those reductions were put into place in 2012, MC, using a conservative -1.5 estimate of the price elasticity of demand, calculated that an additional 12 million broadband connections would be purchased by 2016, and that the loss in ICMS revenues would be only 1.7% in that same year. This estimate did not take into consideration the increase in economic growth that would accompany increased use of broadband.[8] According to studies done at the World Bank, a 10% increase in broadband penetration in developing countries is associated with an increase of 1.4% percentage points in the growth rate of per capita Gross National Product.[9] Had the growth rate increase been included in MC's estimate, the tax reductions would actually result in an increase in ICMS revenues.

Unfortunately, MC's proposal was not accepted. The federal taxes were not reduced and some states even increased the rate of the ICMS. The only reductions were the elimination of the ICMS in a few states on subscriptions to a basic 1 Mbps service offered by some providers under the PNBL. It appears that the federal Ministry of Finance and the state Secretariats of Finance refused to believe in MC's calculations.

At the legislative level, in 2007 a Draft Law (PL 1481/07), allowing the Fust revenues to be used for expanding broadband coverage, was introduced in the Chamber of Deputies. Despite numerous amendments, adjustments, and public hearings, as of February 2014 it was yet to be voted on, reportedly due to opposition from the Ministry of Finance. That ministry continues to use the substantial revenues from this tax of 1% on telephone and Internet service bills to fund interest on the federal government debt. To those who would prefer that it be used for expanding digital inclusion, Fust is called "Frust" (for frustration).

Policies and regulations

Beginning in 2008, but especially since the launch of PNBL and the transfer of responsibility for its implementation to MC in 2011, there have been significant policy reforms and regulations affecting the coverage, cost and quality of Internet connectivity.

The Broadband in Schools program

For primary and secondary education, beginning in 2008 telecommunications operators were required to provide broadband connections at increasing speeds to all urban public schools. This was obtained at virtually no budgetary cost by the so-called "exchange of obligations" agreed in April 2008 whereby the operators were relieved of the requirement to provide thousands of outmoded Telecommunication Services Posts with public phone booths, fax machines and Internet-connected computers. The number of connected public schools tripled to 70,399 by 2013, leaving only 7% of all urban public schools unwired.

Gesac connections, often to remote locations

A program called Electronic Government - Citizens' Support Service (*Governo Eletrônico Serviço ao Cidadão* – Gesac), administered by the MC, was launched during the second administration of President Fernando Henrique Cardoso

(1997-2002) and then transformed and adapted to the policies of the administrations of President Lula (2003-2010). It brings Internet connectivity to telecenters, schools health posts, indigenous communities, military posts, and other institutions, many in remote areas, most initially via satellite, but by landlines as that service becomes available. In October 2013, the number of Gesac installations was 13,379, and should reach some 29,000 in 2014. Some 11,500 new connections will be for health posts and financed by the Ministry of Health.[10]

Licensing of the 450 MHz and 2.5 GHz frequency bands[11]

Operators bidding on 450 MHz frequencies were required to provide voice and data services in rural areas and remote regions as well as free access to rural public schools. By the end of 2015 winning bidders are required to offer these services on a commercial basis within a radius of 30 km from the municipal seat (capital) in all municipalities, thus covering 91% of the rural population as well as to provide free service to all the public schools in these areas, thus serving 96% of public schools. Winners were determined according to the lowest price on commercial connections. In 2012 federal law 12,715 provided a full exemptions from federal taxation for telecommunications services offered on this frequency and for small satellite antennas as well as for network equipment, terminals, and transceivers for these services.

For the 2.5 GHz band, winners in the auction held in June 2012 were required to meet a series of coverage and quality standards. They had to install 4G (Long-Term Evolution – LTE) mobile capacity according to timetables specified in the request for proposals. LTE service was required in the six Confederations Cup cities and was installed by the end of April 2013. Coverage of the 12 World Cup cities by May had to be in place by April 2014 (as of February 2014 this requirement had been met), all cities over 500,000 population by the end of 2015, all municipalities of 30 thousand or more in 2016, 30% of those under 30,000 by the end of 2017, 60% by end of 2018, and 100% by end of 2019.

Domestic content for 3G and 4G equipment has to be 50% of Basic Production Process (*Processo Produtivo Básico* - PPB) value in 2012-2014, rising to 70% in 2017-2022. Technology developed in Brazil has to account for 10% of PPB value in 2012-2014 and increase to 20% in 2017-2022.

Antennas for Mobile Voice and Data Services

Meeting the ambitious federal goals for mobile coverage is hindered by the chaotic system for licensing antennas in urban areas. Licensing a small barely-visible antenna requires fulfilling the same strict requirements as a large one that could have an undesirable visual impact. Licensing is subject to 250 different laws in different municipalities. Operators complain that one of the reasons for poor quality mobile service is that demand has exploded, while licensing new antennas is a complex and slow process. In some municipalities licensing requires approval from seven different agencies. It can take up to 18 months to complete the process. Minister of Communications Paulo Bernardo thinks that it is possible to cut this time to 60 days. Further, the 2.5 GHz band requires four times as many antennas to cover a given area as the not-yet-available 700 MHz band (that will only be free when the transition to digital TV transmission is completed in 2016)

Anatel and MC agreed with the operators in discussions during the June 2013 Rio Wireless conference, though municipal authorities repeated demands for less conspicuous antennas used in major cities abroad, such as London, New York, and Paris. New technologies for almost inconspicuous mini and micro-cell antennas to fill in spaces around more modern widely spaced larger antennas, that are also less of an eyesore, may facilitate this process.

To deal with this problem, a draft General Antennas Law (PL 5013) was approved by the federal Senate in 2013 but as of April 2014 was still proceeding through the Chamber of Deputies. MC is pushing for its approval with urgency, given the approaching deadlines related to the World Cup matches, to begin in June 1914, and the Summer Olympics that will take place in Rio de Janeiro in 2016. In the meantime in Paraná state 76 municipalities have amended their legislation or passed new laws in collaboration with the operators. All but two of the remaining 322 municipalities in Paraná are modifying their legislation, in the process of doing so, or studying the issue.[12]

Freeing up of the part of the 700 MhZ band could be achieved through bringing forward the date that analog broadcasts have to end and only digital signals will be allowed. Digital TV needs less spectrum, and that would allow auctioning some of the freed spectrum for 4G. This is being opposed by the major TV broadcasters on grounds that 4G signals could affect the quality of TV transmissions.

Regulations governing pricing of wholesale bandwidth

MC expects a 30% reduction in the average prices charged for wholesale sales of bandwidth between operators will occur as a result of new regulations introduced by Anatel in 2013. These govern two types of sales: "standard", that is cheaper because the needed infrastructure is already available, and "special" that is more expensive because the needed infrastructure must be built. Previously vaguely defined definitions of "special" allowed operators to charge prices that both their customers and Anatel deemed excessive. Now there are clearer definitions and strict schedules for signing of wholesale contracts, and also new incentives for investments in fiber optic lines, the latter are discussed below.

Regulations governing the quality of broadband service

Beginning in November 2012, fixed broadband providers were required to deliver speeds of at least 20% of the contracted download and upload speeds at any given moment (called instantaneous speed), and 60% of the contracted speed on average as measured over a month. These parameters increased to 30% and 70% in November 2013 and are to reach 40% and 80% in November 2014. Limits on other technical parameters (latency, jitter, and lost packets) were also established for fixed broadband connections. Measurements of average speeds are supposed to be collected by 12,000 volunteers and by public schools using a meter called a "white box". Fines are supposed to levied for violations. Users can test their (instantaneous) speed at any time (e.g. by using the free service at http://www.brasilbandalarga.com.br/speedtest) and report violations.

Despite the new regulations, complaints registered with Anatel increased by 31.1% in 2013 compared with 2012. The fastest growth in complaints was for broadband, 48%.[13]

Tax Incentives for domestic production of modems, tablets, PCs, smartphones and routers (access terminals)

The price of access terminals is the single largest barrier to computer ownership and Internet access by households. CETIC.br's 2012 survey showed that respondents in 63% of residences without a computer gave unaffordable prices as the reason for not purchasing one, with higher numbers for lower-income households, and 44% of households with a computer but no Internet connection indicated that the cost was the reason they had no connection.[14]

For this reason, and also with the objective of encouraging the development of national technology, having a positive impact on the trade balance, and reducing the so-called "grey market" in equipment, the tax rates on access terminals were reduced to zero for the PIS/Cofins and Industrial Products (*Imposto sobre Produtos Industrializados* - IPI) taxes. The MC estimates that for smartphones alone, tax reductions will total R$2 billion (approximately US$830 million) through 2016.

Tax exemptions for PNBL infrastructure (REPNBL-Redes)

The objectives of these measures are to promote investments in broadband infrastructure and promote the national ICT equipment industry. For equipment from domestic producers, exemption from the PIS/Cofins and IPI are granted. For investments in fiber optic networks and other landline and mobile broadband infrastructure, exemptions from PIS/Cofins are granted. Companies must submit their investment projects to the MC. There are domestic content requirements for the equipment used. The MC estimates that these incentives will result in R$3.8 billion (approximately US$ 1.6 billion) in tax reductions thorough 2016. A separate measure established in a law passed in 2011 provides income tax exemptions for individuals and reductions for companies holding debentures financing infrastructure projects.

Progress is evident but much more is needed

A great deal has been accomplished to improve Internet coverage, speed, reduce prices, and improve service quality in recent years, especially since the launch of the PNBL in December 2010. The federal government has indeed given a higher priority to achieving these goals than in the past. There are indications are that it is preparing to do yet more over the coming years, including better funding of the PNBL under a PNBL 2 and faster development of digital cities.[15] Such measures would respond to the needs of the poorer segments of the population and especially the emerging middle class that is demanding more and better public services, but also Internet access at accessible prices. Chapter 8 provides some suggestions for priority actions that could be undertaken by the new Government to be elected in October 2014 and take office in January 2015.

But first Chapters 6 and 7 will look at the dark side of the Internet and Internet governance in Brazil.

Chapter 5: What Is Being Done to Accelerate eTransformation?

1   Secretaria Executiva do Comitê Gestor do Programa de Inclusão Digital (2010), pp 9-10. A collection PNBL documents and presentations is available at http://www4. planalto.gov.br/brasilconectado. Accessed 24 January 2014.

2   http://www.telesintese.com.br/index.php/ plantao/25346-telcomp-cobra-aprovacao-rapida-da-resolucao-dos-postes. Accessed 17 February 2014.

3   For the origins and potential of Eletronet, see Alvim (2007).

4   Correspondence with Michael Stanton, 16 February 2014.

5   Statement by then Telebras President Caio Bonilha at a conference organized by the association of small and medium Internet and telecommunications providers (Abrint) in São Paulo, 14 June 2013.

6   MC (2013).

7   Grizende, Simões da Silva & Stanton (2012).

8   E-Mail correspondence with Pedro Lucas da C. P. Araujo, Project manager, Broadband Department, Secretariat of Telecommunications, Ministry of Communications, 28 June 2013.

9   Qiang & Rossotto (2009), p. 45.

10 Bucco (2013) and MC (2013) http://www.mc.gov.br/ inclusao-digital/noticias/28472-sai-novo-edital-que-vai-expandir-pontos-de-conexao-do-gesac. Accessed 5 February 2014.

11 This section draws heavily on MC (2013).

12 http://www.sinditelebrasil.org.br/sala-de-imprensa/ releases/1545-iniciativa-inedita-no-parana-cria-pacto-para-melhoria-da-qualidade-da-telefonia-movel-no-estado.

13 http://www.anatel.gov.br/consumidor/dados-e-rankings/ and http://www.idec.org.br/em-acao/noticia-consumidor/

reclamaces-na-central-de-atendimento-da-anatel-aumentam-31-no-ano-passado. Both accessed 2 March 2014.

14   CETIC.br (2013), Tables A9 and A 10.

15   http://oglobo.globo.com/tecnologia/pnbl-2-estara-pronto-ate-meio-do-ano-diz-paulo-bernardo-7952990. Accessed 2 March 2014.

Chapter 6

The Dark Side of the Internet

While the benefits of the Internet for economic, social and political development are undeniable, the Internet, like any technology, can be used for good, questionable, illegal, or military purposes. Spam, phishing, child abuse, drug trafficking, piracy of intellectual property, invasions of privacy, terrorism, economic and political espionage by both government agencies and private groups, pervasive surveillance (such as that revealed by Edward Snowden), and cyber warfare are real threats. They can have high costs, for their targets (including time lost and more direct economic losses) and for security measures to defend against them.

Spam and cybercrime

Spam – unsolicited and unwanted e-mail – made up 72.1% of e-mail traffic in 2012, according to Internet security firm Kapersky.[1] Spam has a number of negative impacts including waste of user time, the costs of filtering it where possible, and the clogging of the "pipes" of the Internet with useless or harmful traffic. But spam can also be more dangerous when it includes "phishing" (links to websites purporting to be legitimate, but in practice robbing data, including usernames and passwords to financial institutions). Phishing attacks can also insert viruses or other malware into the user's computer – including code turning it into a "bot" in a clandestine network of thousands of computers manipulated by criminals and hackers to attack other computers or websites. Such networks are called botnets. Child pornography, instructions for making bombs and other weapons of terror are also easily available on the Internet.

Brazil was the largest source of spam in Latin America and the Caribbean in 2012, originating 36.3% of the spam coming from that region and 58.4 of the malicious web pages.[2] The number of Brazilian web servers discovered controlling botnets over the period July 2012 through June 2013 ranged from 4 to 39, with a clear increase in the last four months.[3] Of course Brazil also receives large amounts of spam from the rest of the world including phishing spam.

In September 2011 Symantec released a report by its subsidiary Norton, a major cyber security company. The report estimated the direct cost of global cybercrime: $114 billion annually. Based on the value victims surveyed placed on time lost due to their cybercrime experiences, an additional $274 billion was lost. With 431 million adult victims globally in the past year and at an annual price of $388 billion globally based on financial losses and time lost, cybercrime costs the world significantly more than the global black market in marijuana, cocaine and heroin combined ($288 billion).[4]

The Chief Scientist at the UK Ministry of Defense, Sir Mark Welland, requested a study to identify the main categories of cybercrime and set out what is and is not known of the direct costs, indirect costs, and defense costs – both to the UK and to the world. This request was spurred by the publication in February 2011 of a report commissioned by the UK Cabinet Office that estimated cybercrime's annual cost to the UK to be about $42 billion.[5] For each of the main categories of cybercrime the authors set out what is and is not known of the direct costs, indirect costs and defense costs, both to the UK and to the world as a whole.[6]

The authors observe that we are "extremely inefficient" at fighting cyber crime and offer a hard-line solution: "Our figures suggest that we should spend less in anticipation of cyber crime (on antivirus, firewalls, etc.) and more in response – that is, on the prosaic business of hunting down cyber criminals and throwing them in jail."[7] An August 2012 article in Business Week provides a snapshot of their data illustrating the imbalance between what cyber criminals actually take and the money spent to protect against digital crime. [8] For example, the cost of online banking fraud using phishing or malware was estimated at $690 million (a likely underestimate according to the authors) while the cost of cleaning up infected computers and fighting cyber crime (including firewalls, intrusion detection systems, software maintenance and deployment, and user training) was estimated at some $20 billion, most likely a very conservative estimate.

Brazil is a country with a very advanced banking system that became a world leader in this field during the period of high and hyper-inflation in the 1980s and early 1990s when the ability to move money quickly became urgent. One result was the Brazilian Payments System (*Sistema de* – SPB) for electronic funds transfers.[9] More than 50% of Brazilians use electronic means of communication and computers for financial services, providing an attractive target for organized criminal groups using sophisticated malware for online theft, using false websites appearing to be bank websites to induce unaware bank clients to provide their banking information or divert payments from legitimate transfers (e.g. to pay bills) to the criminals' accounts.[10] According to Trendmicro, in 2013 Brazil had the second largest number of online banking malware detections of any country, exceeded only by the United States.[11]

Privacy, surveillance and the Snowden affair

Privacy issues have been prominent since the early days of the Internet, but have attracted much attention recently. Huge amounts of data are being collected – both for legitimate purposes volunteered by users (e.g. information placed on social networks or obtained by eCommerce firms like Amazon or Netflix) or obtained surreptitiously by national or corporate spy agencies. These data are then analyzed using powerful "big data" techniques.

Edward Snowden was far from the first person to raise the alarm about the potential of pervasive surveillance to create an Orwellian "Big Brother" state. In 2012 Julian Assange, founder of Wikileaks, put it this way in his book *Cypherpunks*:

> "The world is not sliding, but galloping into a new transnational dystopia. This development has not been properly recognized outside of national security circles. It has been hidden by secrecy, complexity and scale. The internet, our greatest tool of emancipation, has been transformed into the most dangerous facilitator of totalitarianism we have ever seen. The internet is a threat to human civilization."[12]

In Brazil, Snowden's revelations, especially concerning surveillance of President Dilma Rousseff and Petrobras, caused great consternation both in the Brazilian Government and in the Internet community. On 16 September 2013, at a meeting in the Planalto Palace, the President requested help from CGI.br in drafting a speech to deliver in the United Nations General Assembly. She delivered the speech on 24 September decrying this surveillance and that of other world leaders. She also declared that Brazil would not only take countermeasures to surveillance, but make proposals for international Internet governance that would "create multilateral mechanisms for the worldwide network that are capable of ensuring principles such as:

1 - Freedom of expression, privacy of the individual and respect for human rights.
2 - Open, multilateral and democratic governance, carried out with transparency by stimulating collective creativity and the participation of society, Governments and the private sector.
3 - Universality that ensures the social and human development and the construction of inclusive and non-discriminatory societies.
4 - Cultural diversity, without the imposition of beliefs, customs and values.
5 - Neutrality of the network, guided only by technical and ethical criteria, rendering it inadmissible to restrict it for political, commercial, religious or any other purposes."[13]

Then on 4 November she issued presidential decree 8135/13 that requires all organs of the federal government to use e-mail, data processing, and datacenters belonging to the federal government.

On November 5, a new version of the draft law on the Civil Rights Framework for the Internet in Brazil (*Marco Civil da Internet –* PL 2126 of 2011) was submitted to the Chamber of Deputies. It reflected the government's concerns aroused by the Snowden affair. Among other changes it introduced a section authorizing the Federal Government to issue a decree requiring ISPs and content providers to store the information of Brazilian users in the country.[14] The MCI and the changes that have been introduced over time are discussed in some detail in Chapter 7.

Cyberwarfare

Cyberwarfare has not only become a potential threat mobilizing huge expenditures for both offensive and defensive measures, but with the Stuxnet attacks on Iranian nuclear facilities, is now a reality. The vulnerability of all kinds of critical systems, including banks, power grids, transportation controls, and military communications is a fact of life, and defending against such threats is both costly and never totally effective. Recent accusations and counter accusations by US and Chinese officials concerning intrusions in government and corporate systems are only the tip of the iceberg. Together with the use of drones, cyberwarfare is revolutionizing military practice. As Tim Hsia and Jared Sperli put it in a New York Times article, "a few thousand lines of code can now be an effective weapon to inflict disarray and damage. But that also means that securing the network is more important than ever, underscored by the publishing of classified military and diplomatic documents by WikiLeaks and the more recent leaks of National Security Agency (NSA) records by Edward J. Snowden."[15]

In sum, like most any technology, the Internet can be used for harmful or evil purposes as well as for positive ones.

Chapter 6: The Dark Side of the Internet

1 www.kaspersky.com/about/news/spam/2013/ Spam_in_2012_Continued_Decline_Sees_Spam_ Levels_Hit_5_year_Low. Accessed 28 January 2014.

2 Trend Micro (2013), pp. 11 and 13.

3 Ibid, p. 14.

4 http://www.symantec.com/about/news/release/article. jsp?prid=20110907 02. Accessed 28 January 2014.

5 Detica and UK Cabinet Office (2011), p. 1.

6 Anderson et al. (2012).

7 Ibid, p. 1.

8 Available at http://www.businessweek.com/articles/ 2012-08-02/the-cost-of-cyber-crime. Accessed 28 January 2014.

9 See Knight & Wanderley (2004).

10 Trend Micro (2013), p. 19.

11 Trend Micro (2014), p. 23.

12 Assange et al. (2012), p. 1 (Location 29 in Kindle edition).

13 The speech can be downloaded at http://gadebate.un.org/ sites/default/files/gastatements/68/BR_en.pdf or viewed at http://www.c-span.org/video/?315200-3/united-nations-general-assembly-speech-brazilian-president-dilma-roussef.

14 See Nazereno (2014) for a balanced discussion of the *Marco Civil* indicating the positions of different stakeholders in its provisions.

15 Hsia & Sperli (2013).

Chapter 7

The Brazilian Model of Internet Governance

This chapter looks at the evolution of the CGI.br, the Civil Rights Framework for the Internet (*Marco Civil da Internet* – MCI), and how these relate to the upcoming NETmundial conference to take place in São Paulo on 23/24 April 2014.

CGI.br Composition and Mandate[1]

The Brazilian Internet Steering Committee (CGI.br), as explained in Chapter 2, was established by Inter-ministerial (MCT and MC) Ordinance 147, of 31 May 1995, later amended by Presidential Decree 4,829 of 3 September 2003. CGI.br is responsible for the coordination and integration of all Internet service initiatives in the country, that is for Internet governance. CGI.br is currently composed of 21 members:

- Nine representatives from the Federal Government
  - Ministry of Science, Technology and Innovation;
  - Ministry of Communication;
  - Presidential Cabinet;
  - Ministry of Defense;
  - Ministry of Development, Industry and Foreign Trade;
  - Ministry of Planning, Budget, and Management;
  - National Telecommunication Agency;

- National Council for Scientific, and Technological Development;
- National Council of State Secretariats for Science, Technology and Information Issues - CONSECTI.
- Four representatives from the corporate sector
  - Internet access and content providers;
  - Telecommunication infrastructure providers;
  - Hardware, telecommunication and software industries;
  - Enterprises that use the Internet.
- Four representatives from the third sector
- Three representatives from the scientific and technological community
- One Internet expert

The mission of the CGI.br involves certain rights and responsibilities, which include:

- proposing policies and procedures regarding the regulation of Internet activities;
- recommending standards for technical and operational procedures for the Internet in Brazil;
- establishing strategic directives related to the use and development of the Internet in Brazil;
- promoting studies and technical standards for network and service security in the country;
- coordinating the allocation of Internet addresses (IPs) and registration in the <.br> domain; and
- collecting, organizing and disseminating information on Internet services, including indicators and statistics.

CGI.br is thus a true multistakeholder body. The federal government is well represented but does not have a majority of voting members. Interestingly, two of the early pioneers of the

Brazilian Internet, whose contributions are discussed in Chapter 2, are members of CGI.br. Demi Getschko holds the Internet expert seat (and is also Chairman of the Executive Board of NIC.br, the executive arm of GCI.br as explained below). Carlos Afonso, a founder of IBASE and Alternex, is one of the representatives of the "third sector", that is civil society organizations or NGOs.

In December 2005, CGI.br created the Brazilian Network Information Center (NIC.br) to serve as the executive arm of the CGI.br. NIC.br's mission involves certain rights and obligations, which include:

- registering and maintaining <.br> domain names, as well as allocating Autonomous System Numbers (ASN) and IPv4 or IPv6 addresses in the country through Registro.br;
- handling and responding to computer security incidents involving networks connected to the Brazilian Internet, which are activities to be carried out by CERT.br;
- projects that support and improve the network infrastructure in the country, such as the direct interconnection between networks (PTT.br) and the distribution of the Brazilian Official Time (NTP.br). These projects are the responsibility of CEPTRO.br;
- producing and publishing indicators, statistics and strategic information on the development of the Brazilian Internet, under the responsibility of CETIC.br;
- promoting studies and recommending procedures, norms and technical and operational standards that will improve network and Internet service security, as well as ensure its increased and adequate use by society, as established by the W3C.br; and
- providing technical and operational support to LACNIC, the Internet Address Registry for Latin America and the Caribbean.

NIC.br's structure is set out in Figure 10.

Figure 10: CGI.br and NIC.br Structure

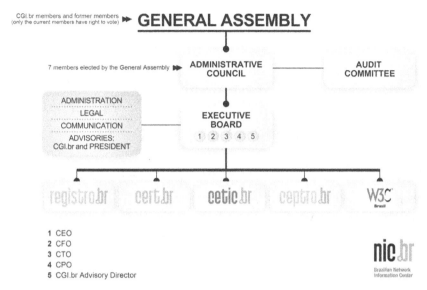

Registro.br – Registry of ".br" domains.

CERT.br – Brazilian National Computer Emergency Response Team

CETIC.br – Center of Studies on Information and Communication Technologies

CEPTRO.br – Center of Study and Research in Network Technology and Operations.

W3C Brasil – The Brazilian office of the W3C (World Wide Web Consortium).

Source: http://www.nic.br/english/about/nicbr.htm

The Civil Rights Framework for the Internet

Building on ten principles developed by CGI.br., a process involving extensive debates in public forums was conducted by the Ministry of Justice and the Getúlio Vargas Foundation. This process culminated in the introduction of a Draft Law (PL 2126/11) in the Chamber of Deputies (lower house of the Brazilian Congress) by president Dilma Rousseff in August 2011. After extensive debates the legislation was passed and signed by the president on 23 April 2014.

The MCI seeks to establish "principles, guarantees, rights, and obligations for the use of the Internet in Brazil". It was subjected to intensive debate in various forums, both before and after being submitted to the Chamber of Deputies. The nature of the debate and drafting were truly participatory, and warrant further examination as a modern democratic process that in many ways is similar to that used in preparing Iceland's draft constitution. The MCI has attracted considerable international attention. It may serve as a model that could be emulated by other countries as well as provide a comprehensive legal framework for Internet governance in Brazil.

The drafting process and debate

In 2009 CGI.br issued a list of ten "Principles for the Governance of the Internet in Brazil". They were:

1. Freedom, privacy and human rights
2. Democratic and collaborative governance
3. Universality
4. Diversity
5. Innovation
6. Neutrality of the network

7. Unaccountability of the network
8. Functionality, security, and stability
9. Standardization and interoperability
10. Legal and regulatory environments.[2]

That same year, a process was initiated to develop a draft law that would eventually become the MCI. The preparation of the pre-draft law was conducted by the Ministry of Justice in partnership with the Technology and Society Center of the Getúlio Vargas Foundation of Rio de Janeiro in two phases, both lasting about 45 days. In the first a white paper with proposed themes and the background was put on a website, www.culturadigital.br/marcocivil, to receive comments. In the second, a pre-draft law was put together based on comments received during the first stage and subjected to the same participatory process. There was also a wiki, a virtual library of references, and a real-time chat forum for open discussion. A hashtag (#marcocivil) and a number of blogs arose spontaneously, further contributing to the debate. The site received over 160,000 visits with more than 2,300 written comments being presented, many of which were taken into consideration in drafting of the law.

On 24 August 2011 president Dilma Rousseff introduced a draft law that resulted from this process in the Chamber, where it became PL 2,126/2011. Between August 2011 and September 2013, 37 other draft laws related to the MCI, some of which were already under consideration and others introduced by deputies, were appended to PL 2,126/2011. The MCI ended up serving as a basic text for a final report that brought together (approving, rejecting, or incorporating) all these other draft laws in a new version of PL 2, 126/2011. Between 6 April and 12 June 2012 seven public hearings were held in six different cities (the first and last were in Brasília). In these hearings, 62 different persons, representing many different and often-conflicting interests and organizations, made formal presentations.

The Internet itself was again used to collect additional comments via the Chamber's site and social media. On July 14, the rapporteur for PL 2126/11 put a draft of his report to the Special Commission on the site for comment, allowing comments through July 16. In those three days the site received 14,673 visits by 3,500 unique visitors and 109 written contributions. Then on 17 July a new version of the draft law was issued. A side-by-side comparison of the full texts of the original, the 17 July 2012, and all subsequent versions is available.[3] Despite several attempts to get the law passed in November and December 2012, no vote was taken that year or during 2013, despite yet another revision of the draft law having been introduced in November of 2013. That revision introduced some new provisions motivated by the furor over Snowden's revelations and sought compromise language on parts of the draft that were most controversial.[4]

Major issues in the debate[5]

The issue that has caused the most polemics is one that has also been the subject of controversy in the United States and Europe: *network neutrality*. The underlying principle of network neutrality is that all Internet traffic should be treated equally, or more specifically, that ISPs should enable access to all content and applications regardless of the source, and without favoring or blocking particular products or websites.

Large telecos and content providers oppose or seek to limit this neutrality not just in Brazil, but all over the world. They claim that they should be able to prioritize certain kinds of traffic to prevent a small number of users (e.g. those downloading high-definition video) from raising costs for other uses and/ or forcing the telcos to make extensive new investments to accommodate this demand. Defenders of network neutrality argue that departing from this principle would result in balkanization of the Internet. Content providers would pay ISPs (mainly the large mostly incumbent telcos) to give priority to their content, putting competitors at a disadvantage. The Internet would become more like cable or satellite TV – the providers could offer different "packages" of content at different prices.

Privacy of personal data – including the maintenance of logs and access to them, the time they must be stored, the use of data obtained from internauts by commercial services (e.g. search engines, social network companies, and e-commerce firms) and where such data is stored – was another area of contention. Finding an acceptable balance between privacy and security resulted in numerous clashes between defenders of privacy and the police, justice system, and commercial interests has proved difficult. This issue became even more contentious following the Snowden revelations.

The requirement to store data obtained from residents of Brazil in the country is an issue that arose when President Dilma sought to include a provision to this effect in the draft after the Snowden revelations. There are cost and feasibility questions raised by this request. A related question is whether connectivity providers and content providers need to be governed by Brazilian legislation, including privacy and personal data, even if the enterprises in question are located outside Brazil.

Intellectual property rights related to content and software piracy and liberty of expression, including access to content containing nudity or sexual acts not authorized by participants, were also the subject of much controversy.

Getting to a vote

On 12 September 2013, President Dilma Rousseff declared PL 2126/11 "urgent". That meant that the Chamber of Deputies had until 28 October to debate, after which no other legislation not also declared urgent could be processed until a vote was taken. She supported the concept of network neutrality but called provisions regarding the storage of data by foreign companies in Brazil, both controversial topics.

The special committee of the Chamber then had to review all other draft laws touching on the subject matter of PL 2126/11 as well as the new contributions to the debate, decide which draft laws and suggestions to accept and which to reject, and then issue a report to the full Chamber that included the final revision of the draft law. This report was issued on 12 February 2014. Finally on 25 March, after some last-minute negotiations that resulted in a broad inter-party agreement, the Chamber of Deputies approved PL 2126/11 almost unanimously. The draft law then went to the Senate, where, under strong pressure from president Dilma, it was approved on the evening of April 22, and then signed by her during the opening ceremony of NETmundial the next day, becoming Law 12,965.

At least one telecommunications specialist has argued that the MCI is not really necessary because it seeks to defend against threats that have not occurred, existing legislation is sufficient or could be modified to achieve legitimate objectives, and attempting to regulate something as dynamic as the Internet could inhibit innovation or simply be ineffective.[6]

Major provisions of the MCI

Law 12,965 incorporates a number of compromises related to the major issues of contention summarized above. Each of these compromises resulted from negotiations influenced by pressures from various stakeholders, often with conflicting interests. The text of the law and can be easily accessed by those interested.[7] The paragraphs that follow summarize how the law deals with these issues.

Net neutrality is guaranteed in Article 9, specifying that "Those responsible for transmission, switching, or routing have the duty to treat equally all data packets, without regard to their content, origin or destination, service, terminal or application." The three paragraphs of Article 1

(a) specify two exceptions to this provision (indispensible technical requirements and priority for emergency services), to be defined (*regulamentada*) by the President of the Republic in accord with a provision of the Federal Constitution and after consulting with CGI.br and Anatel,
(b) set strict principles governing these exceptions, and
(c) prohibit blocking, monitoring, filtering, or analyzing the content of data packets.

This article was the result of strenuous negotiations throughout the entire drafting process that intensified in the last days before approval in the Chamber of Deputies and the Senate. It is a compromise between the interest groups mentioned above.

Privacy of personal data is protected in Articles 10-23, that also specify some exceptions and detail how they will be applied, subject in most cases to judicial orders, unless voluntarily ceded by Internet users. The basic principles governing privacy are set forth in Article 10, that specifies that "The storing and making available of logs regarding the connection and access to Internet applications . . . as well as personal data and the content of private communications should preserve the intimacy, private life, honor, and reputation of the parties directly or indirectly involved." Data collected in Brazil is to be subject to Brazilian law. ISPs must keep logs of user connections and navigation for one year, and limited rights to access to them are specified in great detail. Heavy fines for violating these provisions are set. A campaign by 17 civil society organizations to have the president veto Article 15, that sets the requirements for maintaining and accessing logs that applications providers have to keep, usually for six months (though under judicial order the period can be longer), was not successful.

The requirement to store data obtained from residents of Brazil in the country was not included as part of the law, but Article 11 specifies that in "any operation involving the collection, storage, and processing of logs of personal data or communications by ISPs and application providers, where at least one of these acts occurs in Brazil, must respect Brazilian legislation and rights to privacy, protection of personal data, and the confidentiality of private communications and records."

Intellectual property rights and freedom of expression are protected, subject to provisions regarding libel and offensive material. Article 19, like Article 15 the object of intense controversy, specifies that Internet applications providers will only be held responsible for damage resulting from content generated by third parties if, after a specific judicial order, they do not take measures to, "within the technical limits of their service and within the period indicated, make unavailable the offending content, subject to legal requirements to the contrary." A notice and take down provision requires a judicial order clearly specifying the offending content, except in cases involving posting of images or videos involving nudity or private sexual acts not authorized by the participants after notification by the offended party or parties.

Summing up, the MCI represents the most complete attempt to date, worldwide, to establish a "bill of rights" for Internet users. As it is the result of compromises worked out as competing interest groups or stakeholders pressured the legislators, it exemplifies the definition of politics as the art of the possible. The positions taken by these interest groups during the legislative process also bring to mind the first rule of bureaucratic politics: where you stand depends on where you sit. The battles regarding the major issues of contention will continue as the law is regulated and further defined, including through lawsuits and judicial decisions. The MCI deserves and will get careful study by other countries and the international community as the struggle for improving Internet governance continues.

The evolving international Internet governance ecosystem

The Internet Corporation for Assigned Names and Numbers (ICANN – www.icann.org) was founded in 1998, three years after CGI.br, and is a global multistakeholder organization created and empowered through actions by the U.S. government and its Department of Commerce. ICANN has responsibilities similar to those of CGI.br, but at the international level. It coordinates the Internet DNS, IP addresses, and autonomous system numbers. Carrying out these responsibilities requires continued management of these evolving systems and the protocols that underlie them.

While ICANN has its roots in the U.S. government, it is an international, community-driven organization where all major stakeholders (e.g. ISPs, registries, individual users, commercial and business users, and non-commercial users) are represented on its Board of Directors, elected by their respective constituencies, not by national governments, though governments do have a voice through ICANN's Government Advisory Committee. ICANN manages an interoperable Internet with some 180 million domain names, allocates more than 4 billion network addresses, and supports approximately a trillion DNS look-ups everyday across 240 countries.

Ever since the commercialization of the Internet in the 1990s there has been an ongoing international debate regarding the alleged United States control of the Internet. Not only is ICANN a California corporation, one of its key departments is the Internet Assigned Numbers Authority (IANA – www. iana.org). IANA allocates and maintains unique codes and numbering systems that are used in the protocols that drive the Internet.

IANA dates from the early days of the Internet in the 1970s when it was run by the United States Department of Defense. Today IANA Service Level Targets are defined in part by a contract for IANA performance with the US Department of Commerce, as well as in the Memorandum of Understanding with the Internet Engineering Task Force (IETF), a professional association composed of thousands of engineers and other technical experts. IETF's mission is to make the Internet work better from an engineering point of view.[8]

But on 14 March 2014 the National Telecommunications and Information Administration (NTIA) of the US Department of Commerce announced its intent to transition key Internet domain name functions to the global multistakeholder community. NTIA currently contracts with ICANN to carry out the IANA functions and has a Cooperative Agreement with Verisign, under which it performs related root zone management functions. Transitioning NTIA out of its role marks the final phase of the privatization of the DNS as outlined by the U.S. Government in 1997.

The debate on internationalization of ICANN and IANA and the possible transfer of their functions to the International Telecommunications Union (ITU) – today an agency of the United Nations – has become more heated in recent years in various forums. Among them are ICANN and its constituent bodies themselves, ITU, the Internet Society (ISOC), and the Internet Governance Forum (IGF) that arose out of the World Summit on the Information Society (WSIS) held in two stages in Geneva (2003) and Tunis (2005) under the auspices of the ITU. ICANN is part of a broader Internet ecosystem that involves not only governance, but technical, commercial, and cultural matters, among others, as well. The international, multi-layered, multi-institutional nature of this complex ecosystem is represented in Figure 11.

Figure 11: Layered Model of the Internet Ecosystem

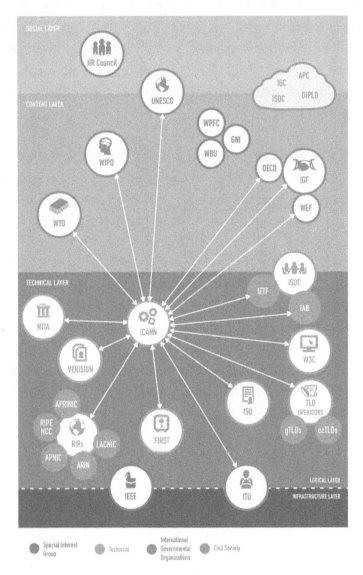

Source: Cerf et al (2014) Figure 7, p. 39

In December 2012 in Dubai, the ITU convened the World Conference on International Communications (WCIT) to review and revise a 1988 treaty called the International Telecommunication Regulations (ITRs). Brazil sided with China,

Russia, Iran, Syria and a number of other less than democratic states in approving a new treaty that was not signed by the United States and 54 other countries from around the world. [9] The disagreement was over language in the ITRs referring to ITU roles in addressing spam and network security, but also and more importantly regarding a resolution on Internet governance that suggests a much more prominent role for governments and the ITU on Internet matters, with only a passing reference to the value and promise of multistakeholder policy development.

Unlike in ICANN, where the controlling Board of Directors is composed of persons representing various constituencies, in the ITU only member states can vote on matters like the ITRs. Thus the ITU is not a multistakeholder organization.

ISOC is a nonprofit organization made up of more than 65,000 members and 91 Chapters worldwide (including a very active one in Brazil). It is dedicated to ensuring the open development, evolution, and use of the Internet for the benefit of all people throughout the world. ISOC – like ICANN, ITEF, many other non-governmental organizations, private sector firms and other constituencies involved in Internet policy making – could only participate in the WCIT as a non-voting member of the ITU.

ISOC believes that "intergovernmental treaty making processes are not the best way address critical Internet policy issues because they do not allow for full multistakeholder engagement in the decision making."[10] ISOC also fears that "the lack of consensus among nations and the persistent aims by some governments to establish Internet policy in a closed, intergovernmental context sets the Internet policy dialogue on uncertain footing. It remains to be seen to what extent the highly politicized environment at the WCIT will permeate future Internet governance discussions."[11]

NETmundial and Brazil

After the Snowden revelations, the debate on Internet governance virtually exploded. The Global Multistakeholder Meeting on the Future of Internet Governance (NETmundial) may be viewed as a new battlefront in what has now been called the Global War for Internet Governance. In a recent book with this title, Laura DeNardis argues that

> "Internet governance is a contested space reflecting broader global power struggles. It is also a twenty-first century reality that Internet governance has expanded beyond operational governance functions. Internet governance technologies are recognized as powerful forces to control the flow of content – for intellectual property rights enforcement, for example. They are also being co-opted for censorship, for surveillance, for kill-switch interventions, and for making political statements via technical mechanisms such as DDoS [Distributed Denial of Service] attacks."[12]

Brazil's hosting of NETmundial is another manifestation of the country's strong reaction to the Snowden affair. Formally NETmundial is an initiative of 1Net (www.1net.org), and organization established after a meeting of global and regional Internet leaders held in Montevideo, Uruguay in October 2013.[13] 1Net is " intended to be a neutral, focused initiative to discuss selected Internet issues with the intent of working towards actionable collaborative solutions"[14] On 7 October 2013 these leaders signed a joint statement known as the Montevideo Statement on the Future of Internet Cooperation. High-level points from the Montevideo Statement include:

- Importance of globally coherent Internet operations;
- Concern over Internet fragmentation at a national level;
- Strong concern over pervasive monitoring and surveillance;
- Ongoing need to address Internet Governance challenges;
- Need for evolution of global multi-stakeholder Internet cooperation;
- Need for globalization of ICANN and IANA functions; and
- Need to allow all stakeholders (including governments) to participate equally.[15]

On October 9, following the Montevideo meeting, ICANN's president, Fadi Chehadé, whose mandate is to accelerate the internationalization of ICANN, met with president Dilma Rousseff in Brasília. After that meeting she announced that Brazil would host what became known as NETmundial. The Minister of Communications, an official of the Ministry of Foreign affairs and two members of CGI.br were given responsibility for organizing the conference.[16]

DeNardis identifies and then discusses a number of unresolved issues at the intersection of Internet governance and Internet freedom in the final chapter of her book. These issues have been discussed extensively in Brazil, especially during the development of the MCI, as well as in the global Internet community. Among them are

> "attempts to introduce government regulation at Internet interconnection points; broader tensions between multistakeholder governance and greater government control; online advertising as a Faustian bargain in which users trade privacy for free Internet goods; the trend away from online anonymity at the technical architecture level; the erosion of Internet interoperability; and

the co-opting of the DNS [Domain Name System] into the Internet's primary content-control mechanism."[17]

These are some of the issues that were hotly debated at the NETmundial conference.

Again quoting from DeNardis' comprehensive study,

> "From a global twenty-first century perspective, Internet freedom is not yet achieved. The same exact technologies that increase possibilities for economic and communicative freedom are also used by governments and private industry to restrict these freedoms. No matter how strenuously media narratives associate social media and other Internet technologies with global political change, there is as much government Internet repression as there are possibilities for Internet political expression. In many parts of the world totalitarian regimes enact surveillance networks of control that limit possibilities for individual privacy and freedom. Even in democratic countries, degrees of Internet freedom related to privacy, expression, and individual autonomy are constantly negotiated against conflicting values of national security and law enforcement."[18]

NETmundial brought together 1,229 participants representing governments, the private sector, civil society, and the scientific/technical community coming from 97 countries. They assembled in São Paulo on 23-24 April 2014. The opening ceremony included president Dilma Roussef, who signed the MCI on the stage after speaking, preceded by Vint Cerf, Tim Berners-Lee, and other key Brazilian and international figures.

The same issues that dominated the debate on the MCI – net neutrality, privacy, and intellectual property rights – were prominent in the almost 200 written comments on a first draft of the NETmundial "Outcomes Document" made available on the Internet only on April 14. This was also the case for hundreds of interventions from the floor by NETmundial participants, from remote hubs around the world with video links to the event, and by e-mails that could be sent from anywhere on the planet. The debates continued during drafting sessions. These sessions were open to observation by participants.

Like the the MCI, the NETmundial Multistakeholder Statement[19] (dubbed by the Brazilian organizers the São Paulo Multistakeholder Declaration) was the product of a bottom-up, open, and participatory process involving thousands of people from governments, the private sector, civil society, the technical community, and academia. But in this case contributions to the drafting process came not only from Brazil, but from around the world.

Also like the MCI, the NETmundial Statement/Declaration embodies numerous compromises that were the result of competing pressures from diverse stakeholders, and hence it left none of them completely satisfied. But the non-binding document was accepted by the overwhelming majority of NETmundial participants as a rough consensus that sets an important benchmark in the ongoing process of globalizing Internet governance that is taking place within different parts of the Internet governance ecosystem (see Figure 11), including the IGF (the mulltistakeholder Internet Governance Forum, that grew out of the WSIS), and the WSIS+10 conference being organized by the ITU.

The 11-page Statement/Declaration is divided into two parts: Internet Governance Principles, and a Roadmap for the future evolution of the Internet Governance Ecosystem.

The principles, some of which are spelled out in bullet points, deal with human rights and shared values; protection of intermediaries; culture and linguistic diversity; unified and unfragmented space; security, stability and resilience of the Internet; open and distributed architecture; enabling environment for sustainable innovation and creativity; Internet governance principles; and open standards. More specific Internet governance principles are spelled out in nine paragraphs with headings being multistakeholder; open, participative, consensus driven governance; transparent; accountable; inclusive and equitable; distributed; collaborative; involving meaningful participation; and access and low barriers.

Net neutrality was hotly disputed and in end not explicitly mentioned in the principles section, though that section does include various expressions that come close to defining the concept. For example, under the heading "unified and unfragmented space" we find "based on a common set of unique identifiers and that allows data packets/information to flow freely end-to-end regardless of the lawful content." In the roadmap section under "Points to be further discussed beyond NETmundial" is the following:

> Net neutrality: there were very productive and important discussions about the issue of net neutrality at NETmundial, with diverging views as to whether or not to include the specific term as a principle in the outcomes. The principles do include concepts of an Open Internet and individual rights to freedom of expression and information.

It is important that we continue the discussion of the Open Internet including how to enable freedom of expression, competition, consumer choice, meaningful transparency and appropriate network management and recommend that this be addressed at forums such as the next IGF.

Privacy of personal data is treated specifically in the principles section under human rights and shared values:

> The right to privacy must be protected. This includes not being subject to arbitrary or unlawful surveillance, collection, treatment and use of personal data. The right to the protection of the law against such interference should be ensured. Procedures, practices and legislation regarding the surveillance of communications, their interception and collection of personal data, including mass surveillance, interception and collection, should be reviewed, with a view to upholding the right to privacy by ensuring the full and effective implementation of all obligations under international human rights law.

Then in the roadmap section there is a rather weak statement regarding surveillance:

> Mass and arbitrary surveillance undermines trust in the Internet and trust in the Internet governance ecosystem. Collection and processing of personal data by state and non-state actors should be conducted in accordance with international human rights law. More dialogue is needed on this topic at the international level using forums

like the Human Rights Council and IGF aiming to develop a common understanding on all the related aspects.

Intellectual property rights are dealt with in the principles section under human rights and shared values:

Freedom of information and access to information: Everyone should have the right to access, share, create and distribute information on the Internet, consistent with the rights of authors and creators as established in law.

This statement was seen by many participants as a victory of major content providers (authors, the film industry, television studios, etc.) over those who view such property as the common intellectual heritage of the human race and seek to curtail existing copyright provisions in national and international law.

The final document was read in the closing plenary session held the evening of April 24. That session began almost three hours late because of continued controversy in the final drafting session. The Statement/Declaration received a standing ovation by most participants. But four participants – representing Russia, India, Cuba and part of the civil society community – then requested the floor. The Russian opposed not only the document, with its emphasis on multistakeholder as opposed to multilateral decision-making (that is, only governments decide, on a one country, one vote basis, as in the UN General Assembly or the ITU), but also the NETmundial process, which he claimed did not take Russian submissions into consideration. The Indian representative said he could not accept the document without consulting his government, while the Cuban claimed that the document did not recognize the role of the United Nations in maintaining peace and a secure, stable and open Internet. The civil society representative said the document did not go far enough to maintain privacy and to prohibit massive online surveillance.

In the roadmap section the decision of the US Government to transition the stewardship of IANA functions to a globalized ICANN and was welcomed and it was recommended that "the discussion about mechanisms for guaranteeing the transparency and accountability of those functions after the US Government role ends, has to take place through an open process with the participation of all stakeholders extending beyond the ICANN community."

The São Paulo declaration's roadmap also argued for strengthening the IGF as a multistakeholder organization that could serve as an appropriate forum for further discussion of Internet governance issues. Specifically it recommended:

a. Improved outcomes: Improvements can be implemented including creative ways of providing outcomes/ recommendations and the analysis of policy options;
b. Extending the IGF mandate beyond five-year terms;
c. Ensuring guaranteed stable and predictable funding for the IGF, including through a broadened donor base, is essential;
d. The IGF should adopt mechanisms to promote worldwide discussions between meetings through intersessional dialogues.

    A strengthened IGF could better serve as a platform for discussing both long standing and emerging issues with a view to contributing to the identification of possible ways to address them.

NETmundial pioneered a process that will likely be emulated and perfected in future events relating not only to Internet Governance, but also to other national and international policymaking efforts. That was recognized in interventions by many of the participants, who also congratulated the organizers of NETmundial for conducting the event in a truly participatory, open manner. At the very end of the final plenary session, someone leapt up and shouted "Thanks to Edward Snowden". Indeed, without his revelations, NETmundial would not have taken place.

Chapter 7: The Brazilian Model of Internet Governance

1   Much of the following text is taken verbatim from the official pages of CGI.br and NIC.br http://www.cgi.br/english/about/definition.htm, http://www.nic.br/english/about/nicbr.htm and related pages.

2   Each principle is succinctly spelled out in the text available at http://cgi.br/regulamentacao/pdf/resolucao-2009-003-pt-en-es.pdf. Accessed 16 February 2014.

3   https://dl.dropboxusercontent.com/u/102898104/CEGO V%20-%202014%20-%20Tabela%20Comparativa%20 Versoes%20Marco%20Civil.pdf. Accessed 19 March 2014.

4   The full record of P 2126/11's passage through the Chamber of Deputies can be found at http://www.camara.gov.br/proposicoesWeb/fichadetramitacao?idProposicao=517255. Accessed 14 February 2014.

5   See Molon (2014) for an exposition on the entire legislative process and the version of PL 2126/11 sent to the Chamber of Deputies in February 2014. The position of the CGI.br as of November 2013 on key elements of the legislation may be found in CGI.br (2013). A good discussion of the principal issues in debate and the changes introduced in the version of 11 November 2013 is DeLuca (2013).

6   Siqueira (2014).

7   See http://www.planalto.gov.br/ccivil_03/_ato2011-2014/2014/lei/l12965.htm. Accessed 29 April 2014.

8   See Molon (2014) and DeLuca (2013) for the full final draft and a discussion of how the major issues were resolved.

9   See ITU (2012) for the Final Acts of the WCIT.

10   Wentworth (2013).

11   Ibid.

12   DeNardis (2014), Chapter 10, Kindle Locations 3780-3784. DeNardis' book is a timely and detailed examination of Internet governance issues.

13   For a detailed description and analysis of NETmundial's gestation, birth and development see Varon (2013).

14   http://1net.org/about. Accessed 15 February 2014.

15   http://www.apnic.net/publications/news/2013/montevideo-statement-on-future-of-internet-cooperation. Accessed 4 March 2014.

16   http://www.cgi.br/acoes/2013/rea-2013-10.htm.

17   DeNardis (2014), Kindle locations 3791-3794.

18   Ibid, Kindle Locations 4147-4153.

19   See http://netmundial.br/wp-content/uploads/2014/04/NETmundial-Multistakeholder-Document.pdf. Accessed 29 April 2014.

Chapter 8

The Future of the Internet in Brazil

ICTs in general and the Internet in particular can benefit countries that can invest in electronic infrastructure, giving users fast, cheap and efficient connections. The importance of a network-interconnected society goes beyond the efficiency gains made possible by powerful devices fed by fiber optic cables and high-speed wireless connections. This electronic infrastructure, however, is only a means – a means to implement an eTransformation strategy for attacking long-standing institutional problems that hold back Brazil's development.

Needed changes in legislation, policies and programs

Previous chapters have mentioned important legislation that has languished in Congress and needs to be passed:

- the General Antennas Law (PL 5013/13) that is needed to accelerate the rollout of 4G wireless service, and
- the MCI (PL 2126/11) that provides a framework of principles, guarantees, rights, and obligations (including for government) for use of the Internet in Brazil.

The MCI needs to be *regulamentado* and this process should involve presentation of the draft provisions online and in public forums for comment, and also be reviewed by Anatel and CGI.

br. It can then provide a guide for other legislation, government programs, and projects.

The LGT already foresaw the need to expand networks and facilitate unbundling. But today the LGT is outdated – it did not foresee the importance of fixed and mobile broadband and while it sought to encourage the universalization of telecommunications services, the emphasis in goals set in the LGT was on fixed-line telephony. While new regulations on wholesale sale of bandwidth and more generally the General Plan for Competitiveness Goals represent advances, the pressure of the large incumbent telcos can make it difficult to enforce these Anatel regulations. While no panacea, a revised LGT could provide a better framework for the development of broadband infrastructure, much as the MCI should for Internet use.

Tax reform at both the federal and state levels is needed for many other purposes, but for Internet development it is critical. Here the priorities should be to eliminate over-taxation of telecommunications equipment and services at the state and federal levels and to end the diversion of Fust and Fistel tributes to financing the primary surplus.

Two challenges

Brazil faces two Internet challenges: keeping pace with rapid advances outside Brazil and making accelerated broadband infrastructure development part of a broad eTransformation strategy.

Today, another new wave of innovation is being powered by Big Data, analytics, mobile, social and cloud computing. The environment is moving from monolithic applications to dynamic services; from structured data at rest to unstructured data in motion; from PCs to unprecedented numbers and kinds of devices; from stable to unpredictable workloads; from static infrastructure to cloud services; and from proprietary standards to open innovation. Taking advantage of these innovations will require better broadband infrastructure.

The PNBL is an important advance in developing this infrastructure. But Brazil must do more than this. The challenge of improving Internet connectivity is part of a broader challenge of increasing investment in education, health, public safety and physical infrastructure needed to continue advancing social justice and enable Brazil to play a relevant and constructive role in the world economy. The expected PNBL 2.0 should to be incorporated into a broader eTransformation strategy, currently missing, to achieve major synergies across government agencies and programs to realize improvements in socioeconomic development, political participation, and competitiveness that Brazil requires to become a first world global power.

Consensus formation

Brazil is on the right path. But a more holistic approach supported by a broader consensus about the strategic importance of the Internet for the country's economic, social, and political development is needed. Building this consensus is necessary to obtain political support – not only for accelerated buildout of broadband connectivity but also for an eTransformation strategy as a central thrust Brazil's overall development policies.

The absence of this kind of political consensus was starkly revealed as the drafting of this book was nearing completion in mid-February 2014. A major party in the government coalition threatened to vote against the Civil Rights Framework for the Internet in Brazil unless the party's demands for more ministerial posts in President Rousseff's lame duck pre-election cabinet were met. While there were some members of that party who opposed parts of the legislation on substantive grounds of the legislation, the threat was to vote against all urgent legislation, not just the MCI, simply as blackmail to obtain ministerial posts in an election year.

The imminence of NETmundial may provide an opportunity for helping build this needed consensus. For this to happen, Brazil's print and electronic media must become seriously engaged in this struggle. Specialized journalists and CGI.br can help mobilize needed coverage.

Television remains the predominant communication medium in Brazil: 97% of homes had a color TV set in 2012,[1] while only 40% had a computer with Internet access.[2] According to a survey by polling firm IBOPE, the average hours per day spent watching television in 2013 was five hours and 45 minutes.[3] Print media penetration is less: in the last nine days prior to an IBOPE survey, 31% of the population had read a newspaper and 36% a magazine.[4] Television formats – including news, "magazines" like TV Globo's *Globo Reporter* or *Fantástico*, interviews, and dramatic serials (*telenovelas* and mini-series) – can all be used to promote greater awareness of the Internet's importance for individuals, families, cities, enterprises, and better government services.[5]

Final thoughts

Brazil is favored by generous endowments of natural resources, a dynamic agro-industrial sector, a nearly complete industrial structure, a rapidly growing service sector, and a creative population. This population is passing through a demographic transition, but is still relatively young and flexible. High-speed Internet connectivity is essential for Brazil to solve long-standing social problems and realize its full development potential, meet its citizen's demands for a better life, and contribute to solving 21st century global problems.

Achieving these objectives is feasible. But it will require inspired leadership and a clear strategy to take advantage of the ICT revolution.

Chapter 8: The Future of the Internet in Brazil

1   http://www.sidra.ibge.gov.br/bda/tabela/protabl.
     asp?c=1954&z=pnad&o=3&i=P. Accessed 17 February 2014.
2   http://www.cetic.br/usuarios/tic/2012/A4.html. Accessed
     17 February 2014.
3   http://www.ibope.com.br/pt-br/noticias/Paginas/Leitura-
     de-jornal-e-maior-na-Colombia-e-na-Guatemala-aponta-
     Media-Book-2013.aspx. Accessed 17 February 2014.
4   http://www.ibope.com.br/pt-br/noticias/Paginas/Leitura-
     de-jornal-e-maior-na-Colombia-e-na-Guatemala-aponta-
     Media-Book-2013.aspx. Accessed 17 February 2014.
5   Knight & Schiavo (2007).

References

Akami, (2014). *The State of the Internet: Third quarter 2013 Report.* 6:3. http://www.akamai.com/dl/akamai/akamai-soti-q313.pdf?WT.mc_id=soti_Q313. Accessed 29 January 2014.

Almeida, M. (2013). "Em três anos, 48 mil lan houses fecham as portas no Brasil". IG, Economia: Seu Negócio, 11 October. http://economia.ig.com.br/financas/seunegocio/2013-10-11/em-tres-anos-48-mil-lan-houses-fecham-as-portas-no-brasil.html. Accessed 9 February 2014.

Alvim, M. (2007). "Eletronet: um enigma das telecomunicações – sua viabilidade para o desenvolvimento nacional". Chapter 16 in Knight, Fernandes & Cunha (2007), pp 374-393.

Anatel (2013). *Relatório Anual 2012.* Brasília: Anatel.

Anatel (2012). *Relatório de Gestão do Exercício 2011: Fundo de Universalização dos Serviços de Telecomunicações.* Brasília: Anatel.

Anderson, R., Barton, C. Böhme, R., Clayton, R., van Eeten, M. J. G., Levi, M.....Savage, S. (2012). "Measuring the Cost of Cybercrime", WEIS. http://weis2012.econinfosec.org/papers/Anderson_WEIS2012.pdf. Accessed 6 February 2014.

Assange, J., Appelbaum, J. Müller-Maguhn, A. & Zimmermann, J. (2012). *Cypherpunks: Freedom and the Future of the Internet.* New York and London: OR Books, Kindle Edition (2013).

Assumpção, R. & Falavigna, M. (2004). "Sampa.org: Um projeto de inclusão digital". Chapter 9.1 in Chahin, Cunha, Knight & Pinto (2004), pp. 254-268.

Assumpção, R. & Mori, C. (2007). "Inclusão digital: Discursos, práticas e um longo caminho a percorrer." Chapter 19 in Knight, Fernandes & Cunha (2007), pp. 431-442.

Baer, W. (2001). *The Brazilian Economy: Growth and Development.* Fifth Edition. Westport, CT: Praeger.

Baggio, R. & De Luca, C. (2004). Escolas de informática, cidadania e inclusão digital." Chapter 9.2 in Chahin, Cunha, Knight & Pinto (2004), pp. 261-268.

Baran, P. (1964). "On Distributed Communications: I. Introduction to Distributed Communications Networks". Memorandum RM-3420-PR. Santa Monica, California: The RAND Corporation. August. http://www.rand.org/content/dam/rand/pubs/research_memoranda/2006/RM3420.pdf. Accessed 12 March 2014.

Bilbat-Osorio, B., Dutta, S., & Lavin, B. (eds.) (2013). *The Global Information Technology Report 2013: Growth and Jobs in a Hyperconnected World.* Geneva: INSEAD and World Economic Forum.

Brazilian Internet Steering Committee, CETIC.br (2013). *ICT Households and Enterprises 2012.* São Paulo: CGI.BR. This report and all earlier editions and special reports beginning in 2005 are downloadable in pdf format at http://www.cetic.br/publicacoes/index.htm. Tables for 2012 are available at http://www.cetic.br/usuarios/tic/2012/index.htm.

Bucco, R. (2013) "Minicom promete 24 mil novos postos Gesac em 2014". *A Rede* December 2. http://www.arede.inf.

br/noticias/6399-minicom-promete-24-mil-novos-pontos-gesac-em-2014. Accessed 5 February 2014.

Castells, M. (2010). *The Rise of the Networked Society.* Second Edition, with a new preface. New York: Wiley-Blackwell.

Castells, M. (2012) *Networks of Outrage and Hope: Social Movements in the Internet Age.* Cambridge, UK: Polity Press.

Castro, D. (2014). "Brasileiro mais pobre passa mais de um quarto do dia vendo televisão". http://noticiasdatv.uol.com.br/noticia/audiencias/brasileiro-mais-pobre-passa-mais-de-um-quarto-do-dia-vendo-televisao-1840 13 January. Accessed 17 February 2014.

Chahin, A., Cunha, M. A., Knight, P. T. & Pinto, S. L. (2004). *E-Gov.br: A próxima revolução Brasileira – Eficiência, qualidade e democracia: o governo eletrônico no Brasil e no mundo.* São Paulo: Prentice Hall.

Cerf, V. (Chair) et al. (2014). "ICANN's Role in the Internet Governance Ecosystem," Report of the ICANN Strategy Panel, February 20. http://www.icann.org/en/about/planning/strategic-engagement/governance-ecosystem/report-23feb14-en.pdf. Accessed 4 March 2014.

Comitê Gestor do Programa de Inclusão Digital – CGPID, Secretaria Executiva (2010). *Brasil Conectado, Programa Nacional de Banda Larga* (Brasília: Presidência da República, http://www4.planalto.gov.br/brasilconectado/forum-brasil-conectado/documentos/3o-fbc/documento-base-do-programa-nacional-de-banda-larga. Accessed 24/01/2014.

CGI.br (2013). *O CGI.br e O Marco Civil da Internet: Defesa da privacidade de todos que utilizam a Intrernet; Neutralidade da*

rede; Inimputabilidade da rede. São Paulo: CIG.br. http://www.
cgi.br/publicacoes/documentacao/CGI-e-o-Marco-Civil.pdf.
Accessed 4 March 2014.

Coelho, F. D. (2007). "Cidades Digitais: Caminhos de um programa
nacional de inclusão digital". Chapter 27 in Knight, Fernandes &
Cunha (2007), pp. 460-488.

Comscore (2013). "Brazil: Digital Future in Focus: Key Insights
for 2012 and what they mean for the coming year". March.
http://www.slideshare.net/idegasperi/dados-comscore-2013-
sobre-o-comportamento-brasil. Accessed 31 January 2014.

Conner, M. (2012). Data on Big Data. 18 July. http://marciaconner.
com/blog/data-on-big-data/. Accessed 29 January 2014.

Considera, C. M., Franco, F. L., Saintive, M. B., Teixeira, C. P., Pinheiro,
M. C., Moraes, R. K. ....Soares, D. P. (2002). "O Modelo Brasileiro
de Telecomunicações: Aspectos concorrenciais e regulatórios".
August. https://gestaoseae.fazenda.gov.br/central_documentos/
documento_trabalho/2002-1/doctrab18.pdf. Accessed 16 April
2014

Dantas, V. (1988). *Guerrilha Tecnológica: A verdadeira história
da política nacional de informática.* Rio de Janeiro & São Paulo:
Livros Técnicos e Científicos.

DeLuca, C. (2013). Marco Civil: entenda o que mudou com a nova
redação". http://idgnow.com.br/blog/circuito/2013/11/05/
marco-civil-entenda-o-que-mudou-com-a-nova-
redacao/#sthash.aRDLq8CF.dpuf. Accessed 12 February 2014.

DeNardis, L. (2014). *The Global War for Internet Governance.* New
Haven and London: Yale University Press. Kindle Edition.

Detica & UK Cabinet Office (2011). *The Cost of Cybercrime: A Detica Report in Partnership with the Office of Cyber Security and Information Assurance in the Cabinet Office*. Guildford, Surrey, UK: Detica. https://www.gov.uk/government/uploads/system/uploads/attachment_data/file/60943/the-cost-of-cyber-crime-full-report.pdf. Accessed 6 February 2014.

Falavinha, M. (2011). *Inclusão Digital: Vivências brasileiras*. São Paulo: IPSO - Instituto de Projetos e PesquisasSociais e Tecnológicas. http://www.scribd.com/doc/73749199/Mauricio-Falavigna-Inclusao-Digital-Vivencias-Brasileiras-Web-Version#download. Accessed 16 April 2014

Federação Brasileira de Bancos – FEBRABAN (2012). "Tecnologia para Acelerar." CIAB Febraban. December. http://www.ciab.com.br/_pdfs/publicacoes/2012/43-Dez2012.pdf. Accessed 25 June 2013.

Galitsky, A. V., Knight, P. T., Tichonov, M. E., Chapljgin & Volipov, A. V. (1994). Network Infrastructure Development and Defense Industry Conversion for Satellite Towns: Using and Building an Electronic Distance Education System for Russia with Connections to the Worldwide Information Society. Moscow: Proceedings of the Second International Conference on Distance Education in Russia. http://web.archive.org/web/20021229152224/http://knight-moore.com/pubs/pubsindex.htm. Accessed 24 February 2014.

Gantz, J. & Reinsel, D. (2012). "The Digital Universe In 2020: Big Data, Bigger Digital Shadows, and Biggest Growth in the Far East". IDC report for EMC, December. http://idcdocserv.com/1414. Accessed 29 January 2014.

Gazzarrini, R (2013). "Brasil: vendas de smartphones batem recorde no terceiro trimestre de 2013" Tecmundo 28 November.

http://www.tecmundo.com.br/celular/47627-brasil-vendas-de-smartphones-batem-recorde-no-terceiro-trimestre-de-2013.htm#ixzz2rvIn4yqi. Accessed 30 January 2014.

Ghonim, W. (2012). *Revolution 2.0: The Power of the People is Greater than the People in Power – a Memoir.* New York and Boston: Houghton.

Grizendi, E., Simões da Silva, N. & Stanton, M. (2012). "Brazilian experience of connecting at 100 Mb/s and 1 Gb/s universities and researcher institutions in the interior of the country". Proceedings and report of the 5th UbuntuNet Alliance annual conference, ISSN 2223-7062, Dar es Salaam, Tanzania 15-16 November.

Grizende, E. & Stanton, M. (2013). "Use of Subfluvial Optical Cable in a Region Without Land-Based Infrastructure – a Project to Deploy Advanced Communications in the Amazon Region". *Proceedings and reports of the 6th UbuntuNet Alliance annual conference, 2013*, pp 53-68. http://www.ubuntunet.net/sites/ubuntunet.net/files/grizend.pdf. Accessed 7 February 2014.

Haffner, K. & Lyon, M. (1996). *Where Wizards Stay Up Late: The Origins of the Internet.* New York: Touchstone.

Hanna, N. K. & Knight, P. T. (eds). (2011). Seeking Transformation Through Information Technology: Strategies for Brazil, China, Canada and Sri Lanka. New York: Springer.

Hanna, N. K & Knight, P. T. (eds.). (2012). *National Strategies to Harness Information Technology: Seeking Transformation in Singapore, Finland, the Philippines, and South Africa.* New York: Springer.

Hsia, T. & Sperli (2013). "How Cyberwarfare and Drones Have Revolutionized Warfare". International New York Times. June

17. http://atwar.blogs.nytimes.com/author/tim-hsia-and-jared-sperli/. Accessed 6 February 2014.

Hutchinson, J. (2013). "McAfee regrets 'flawed' trillion dollar cybercrime claims. *Financial Review* 19 August. http://www.afr.com/p/technology/mcafee_regrets_ flawed_trillion_dollar_msQ2WFkVLEZKx7Yv7ZCMQI. Accessed 6 February 2014.

IBOPE Inteligência (2013). *ICS – Índice de Confiança Social 2013*. http://www.ibope.com.br/pt-br/noticias/paginas/cai-a-confianca-dos-brasileiros-nas-instituicoes-.aspx. Accessed 24/02/2014.

Instituto Brasileiro de Geografia e Estatística – IBGE (2013). *Pesquisa Nacional Por Amostra de Domicílios 2012*. Rio de Janeiro: IBGE.

International Telecommunications Union – ITU (2012). *Final Acts of the World Conference on International Telecommications*. Dubai: ITU. Downloadable at http://www.itu.int/en/wcit-12/ Documents/final-acts-wcit-12.pdf. Accessed 15 February 2014.

International Telecommunications Union – ITU (2013). *Measuring The Information Society 2013*. Geneva, ITU. http://www.itu. int/en/ITU-D/Statistics/Documents/publications/mis2013/ MIS2013_without_Annex_4.pdf. Accessed 17 April 2014.

Jensen, M. (2011). *Broadband in Brazil: A Multipronged Public Sector Approach to Digital Inclusion*. Washington, D.C.: Infodev.

Kleinrock, L (1961). "Information Flow in Large Communication Nets", *RLE Quarterly Progress Report*, July.

Kleinrock, L. (1964). *Communication Nets: Stochastic Message Flow and Delay*. New York: Mcgraw-Hill.

Knight, P. T. & Fernandes, C. C. C. (2006). *e-Brasil: Um programa para acelerar o desenvolvimento socioeconômico aproveitando a convergência digital*. São Caetano do Sul, São Paulo: Yendis.

Knight, P. T., Fernandes, C. C. C, & Cunha, M. A. (eds.). (2007). *E-Desenvolvimento no Brasil e no mundo: Subsídios e Programa e-Brasil*. São Caetano do Sul, São Paulo: Yendis.

Knight, P. T. & Schiavo, M. R. (2007). "Desenvolvimento de um consenso nacional". Chapter 11 in Knight, Fernandes & Cunha (2007), pp 273-291.

Knight, P. T. & Annenberg, D. (2008). "Brazil's Experience with Integrated Citizen Service Centers. PowerPoint Presentation at Zelenograd Prefecture. Moscow Oblast, Russian Federation, 28 May.

Knight, P. T. & Wanderley, C. A. (2004). "O Sistema de Pagamentos Brasileiro (SPB)". Chapter 4.4 in Chahin, Cunha, Knight & Lemos (2004).

Knight, P. T. (2008). "Argumentos econômicos em favor do e-desenvolvimento". *Revista de Economia & Relações Internacionais*. 6:12, January, pp 81-102. http://www.faap.br/revista_faap/rel_internacionais/pdf/revista_economia_12.pdf. Accessed 25/01/2014

Knight, P. T. (2013). "The Internet in Brazil: Poor strategy weakens progress". *Braudel Papers* No. 48. São Paulo. 25/01/2014. http://en.braudel.org.br/publications/braudel-papers/48.php. Accessed 17 April 2014.

Lunden, I. (2013). "Mobile Data Traffic To Grow 300% Globally By 2017 Led By Video, Web Use, Says Strategy Analytics". July 3. http://techcrunch.com/2013/07/03/mobile-data-use-to-grow-300-globally-by-2017-led-by-video-web-traffic-says-strategy-analytics/ Accessed 25/01/2014

Markoff, J. (2013). "Viewing where the Internet Goes". New York Times, 31 December, p. D5. http://www.nytimes.com/2013/12/31/science/viewing-where-the-internet-goes.html Accessed 15 February 2014.

Mattos, C. (2014). "Por que custa caro ligar de telefone fixo para celular". Brasil: Economia e Governo, February 4. http://www.brasil-economia-governo.org.br/2014/02/04/por-que-custa-caro-ligar-de-telefone-fixo-para-celular/#respond. Acessed 24 February 2014.

Menezes de Carvalho, M. S. R. (2006). *A Trajetoria da Internet no Brasil: Do surgimento das redes de computadores à institucionalização dos mecanismos de governança*. M.Sc. dissertation in Engineering and Computer Systems, Federal University of Rio de Janeiro (COPPE/UFRJ). September.

Ministério das Comunicações (MC) (2013). "Programa Nacional de Banda Larga PNBL Situação em Junho de 2013". Powerpoint Presentation.

Molon, A. (2014). *Substitutivo Oferecido em Plenário em Substituição à Comissão Especial Destinada a Proferir Parecer ao Projeto de Lei N° 2016 de 2011, do Poder Executivo, que "Estabelece Princípios, garantias, direitos e deveres para o uso da Internet no Brasil"*. Brasília: Câmara dos Deputados. http://www.camara.gov.br/proposicoesWeb/prop_mostrar

integra?codteor=1225789&filename=Parecer-PL212611-12-02-2014. Accessed 14 February 2014.

Mundy, S. (2014). "Global Smartphone Sales Top 1bn in 2013, shoes IDC Report". *Financial Times*, January 28.

Nazereno, C. (2014). *Texto de Referência Acerca do Marco Civil da Internet para o 'Fique por Dentro'*. Nota Técnica. Brasília: Consultoria Legislativa. http://www2.camara.leg.br/documentos-e-pesquisa/fiquePorDentro/temas/marco-civil/texto-base-da-consultoria-legislativa-pdf. Accessed 12 February 2014.

Paganini, P. (2013). "2013 – The Impact of Cybercrime". Infosec Institute, November 1. http://resources.infosecinstitute.com/2013-impact-cybercrime/. Accessed 6 February 2014.

Peregrino, F. and Porto, T. (2004). "Infovia.RJ: O novo caminho da Internet no Rio de Janeiro." Chapter 10.1 in Chahin et al., pp294-304.

Ramires, E. (2014). "A neutralidade e o futuro das redes de banda larga". *Valor Econômico*, 11 February.

Qiang, C. Z. & Rossotto, C. M. (2009). "Economic Impacts of Broadband". Chapter 3 in World Bank (2009), pp. 35-50. http://siteresources.worldbank.org/EXTIC4D/Resources/IC4D_Broadband_35_50.pdf. Accessed 17 April 2014.

Schumpeter, Joseph A (1950). *Capitalism, Socialism, and Democracy*, Third Edition. New York: Harper and Row.

Schwab, K. (2013). *Global Competitiveness Report 2013-2014*. Geneva: World Economic Forum.

Siqueira, E. (2014). "Para entender o polêmico Marco Civil da Internet". http://www.telequest.com.br/portal/index.php/destaque/1182-para-entender-o-polemico-marco-civil-da-internet. Accessed 17 April 2014.

Slater, W. F. III (2002). "Internet History and Growth". Presentation to the Chicago Chapter of the Internet Society. http://www.internetsociety.org/sites/default/files/2002_0918_Internet_History_and_Growth.ppt. Accessed 25/01/2014

Smith, A. (2011). *An Inquiry into the Nature and Causes of The Wealth of Nations*. ISBN 978-1-937810-33-7. Seedbox Press, LLC. Kindle Edition. First published 1776.

Stanton, M. (1993). "Non-Commercial Networking in Brazil". Proceedings INET 1993. pp GFB1-GFB10.

Stanton, M, Machado, I, Faerman, M, Moura, A. L., Brauner, D. F., Marins, A., Doelho, T. & Rodríguez, N. (2010). "RNP: A Brief Look at the Brazilian NREN". Presented at Terena Networking Conference (TNC2010) Vilnius, Lithuania. Published in TNC 2010 – Living the Network Life. Vol.1. Amsterdam: Trans-European Research and Education Networking Association.

Symantic (2013). "Relatório Norton 2013: Custo por Vítima do Cibercrime cresce 50%". October 2. http://www.symantec.com/pt/br/about/news/release/article.jsp?prid=20131002_01. Accessed 6 February 2014.

Takahashi, T. (ed.). (2000). *Sociedade da Informação no Brasil: Livro Verde*. Brasília: Ministério da Ciência e Tecnologia.

September. Available for download at http://www.mct.gov.br/index.php/content/view/18878.html. Accessed 23/01/2014.

Takahashi, T. (2007). "Rumo a um e-Brasil: pontos a ponderar". Chapter 10 in Knight, Fernandes & Cunha(2007), pp 222-272.

Telebrasil (2013). *Desempenho do Setor de Telecomunicações no Brasil. Séries Temporais. 2012.* Rio de Janeiro: Telebrasil, April

Thorvaldur, G. (2013). "Democracy on ice: a post-mortem of the Icelandic constitution". http://www.opendemocracy.net/can-europe-make-it/thorvaldur-gylfason/democracy-on-ice-post-mortem-of-icelandic-constitution. Accessed 18 February 2014.

Toledo, Paulo F. (2004). "Inclusão digital: Uma proposta empreendedorista". Chapter 9.3 in Chahin, Cunha, Knight & Pinto (2004), pp. 269-277.

Trend Micro (2013). "Brasil: Desafios de Segurança Cibernética Enfrentados por uma Economia em Rápido Crescimento" http://www.trendmicro.com.br/cloudcontent/br/pdfs/home/wp-brasil-final.pdf. Accessed 6 February 2014.

Trend Micro (2014). *TrendLabs 2013 Annual Security Roundup: Cashing in on Digital Information – An Onslaught of OnlineBanking Malware and Ransomware.* http://housecall.trendmicro.com/cloud-content/au/pdfs/security-intelligence/reports/rpt-cashing-in-on-digital-information.pdf. Accessed 12 February 2014.

Varon, J. F. (2013). Conferência Multissetorial Global sobre o Futuro da Governança da Internet: o que é? de onde veio? para onde vai?" http://observatoriodainternet.br/conferencia-multissetorial-global-sobre-o-futuro-da-governanca-da-internet-o-que-e-de-onde-veio-para-onde-vai. 28 November. Accessed 4 March 2014.

Wentworth, S. S. (2013). "Testimony to the House of Representatives on the results of WCIT". http://www.internetsociety.org/doc/WCIT_hor_testimony. Accessed 15 February 2014.

Wilgren, M. (2013). "The Birth and Death of Big Data". The Data Center Journal. 29 April. http://www.datacenterjournal.com/it/birth-death-big-data/#!prettyPhoto. Accessed 29 January 2014.

World Bank (2009). *Information and Communications for Development: Extending Reach and Increasing Impact*. Washington DC: World Bank.

Zweig, S. (1943). *Brazil: Land of the Future*. New York: Viking Press. Original published in German in 1941 as *Brasilien, Ein Land der Zukunft*

About the Author

Peter T. Knight is an economist specialized in the use of information and communication technologies for accelerating economic, social, and political development. A resident of Rio de Janeiro, he is a founding member, researcher, and member of the Board of Directors of the Fernand Braudel Institute of World Economics in São Paulo.

Peter holds a Ph.D from Stanford University and degrees in Government from Dartmouth College and Politics, Philosophy and Economics from Oxford University. He has worked at the Center for Training and Research on Economic Development (Rio de Janeiro), Brookings Institution (Washington DC), Ford Foundation (Lima Peru), Cornell University, and the World Bank, where he was Lead Economist for Brazil, Chief of the National Economic Management Division of the Economic Development Institute, and Chief of the Electronic Media Center.

During his 20 years at the World Bank he led pioneering studies on Brazil dealing with poverty and basic needs, economic stabilization, and macroeconomic analysis of financial systems. At the Electronic Media Center he produced 15 documentary television programs and videos focusing on the use of information and communication technologies for development and supported the production of two Russian feature documentaries and a ten-episode dramatic serial broadcast on nationwide TV networks. He was a co-organizer of two international conferences on distance education held in Moscow. After graduating from the World Bank in 1997 he has worked as a consultant in South

Africa, Zimbabwe, Qatar, Pakistan, Bahrain, Russia and several Brazilian states.

A well-known Brazilianist, he is the author and/or editor of nine previous books on Brazil in English and Portuguese and almost of over 150 books, chapters in other books, articles, and World Bank reports. He was the general coordinator of the e-Brasil Project that brought together 70 Brazilian and international authors who collaborated to produce a 40 chapter book on eDevelopment in Brazil and the world that won a coveted Jabutí prize from the Brazilian Chamber of Books in 2008.

Born in Cleveland, Ohio, Peter speaks fluent French, Portuguese, Spanish and passable Russian.

Index

www.ingramcontent.com/pod-product-compliance
Lightning Source LLC
Chambersburg PA
CBHW021142070326
40689CB00043B/1003